W9-DEE-820

Should Juveniles Be Tried as Adults?

Should Juveniles Be Tried as Adults?

Other books in the At Issue series:

Affirmative Action
Are Efforts to Reduce Terrorism Successful?
Are the World's Coral Reefs Threatened?
Club Drugs
Do Animals Have Rights?
Does the World Hate the United States?
Do Infectious Diseases Pose a Serious Threat?
Do Nuclear Weapons Pose a Serious Threat?
The Ethics of Capital Punishment
The Ethics of Euthanasia
The Ethics of Genetic Engineering
The Ethics of Human Cloning
Fast Food
Food Safety
Gay and Lesbian Families
Gay Marriage
Gene Therapy
How Can School Violence Be Prevented?
How Should America's Wilderness Be Managed?
How Should the United States Withdraw from Iraq?
Internet Piracy
Is Air Pollution a Serious Threat to Health?
Is America Helping Afghanistan?
Is Gun Ownership a Right?
Is North Korea a Global Threat?
Is Racism a Serious Problem?
The Israeli-Palestinian Conflict
Media Bias
The Peace Movement
Reproductive Technology
Sex Education
Teen Suicide
Treating the Mentally Ill
UFOs
What Energy Sources Should Be Pursued?
What Motivates Suicide Bombers?
Women in the Military

Should Juveniles Be Tried as Adults?

Judy Layzell, *Book Editor*

Bruce Glassman, *Vice President*
Bonnie Szumski, *Publisher*
Helen Cothran, *Managing Editor*

GREENHAVEN PRESS
An imprint of Thomson Gale, a part of The Thomson Corporation

Detroit • New York • San Francisco • San Diego • New Haven, Conn.
Waterville, Maine • London • Munich

For more information, contact
Greenhaven Press
27500 Drake Rd.
Farmington Hills, MI 48331-3535
Or you can visit our Internet site at http://www.gale.com

LIBRARY OF CONGRESS CATALOGING-IN-PUBLICATION DATA

Should juveniles be tried as adults? / Judy Layzell, book editor.
   p. cm. — (At issue)
Includes bibliographical references and index.
ISBN 0-7377-1977-X (lib. : alk. paper) — ISBN 0-7377-1978-8 (pbk. : alk. paper)
   1. Juvenile delinquents—United States. 2. Prosecution—United States.
3. Criminal liability—United States. I. Layzell, Judy. II. At issue (San Diego, Calif.)
KF9812.S54 2005
345.73'04—dc22
                                      2004047463

Contents

		Page
Introduction		8
1. Trying Juveniles as Adults Is Unconstitutional *Mike Clary*		14
2. Trying Juveniles as Adults Is Immoral *Terence T. Gorski*		22
3. Sanctioning Youths as Adults Has Broad Public Support *Daniel P. Mears*		27
4. The Juvenile Justice System Is Too Lenient on Violent Offenders *Linda J. Collier*		39
5. Juvenile Offenders Are Endangered in Adult Facilities *Brian Hansen*		45
6. Transferring Juveniles to Adult Court Does Not Deter Crime *Harry Shorstein et al.*		49
7. Minority Youth Are Disproportionately Represented in Adult Court *Jolanta Juszkiewicz*		56
8. Severe Measures Are Necessary to Protect Citizens from Juvenile Criminals *John Ashcroft*		72
9. Juvenile Offenders Have Been Unfairly Demonized *Linda S. Beres and Thomas D. Griffith*		77
10. Lack of Brain Development Makes Juveniles Less Culpable than Adults *Adam Ortiz*		92
Organizations to Contact		100
Bibliography		103
Index		105

Introduction

In 1992, fifteen-year-old Jose Martinez and two older companions tortured and decapitated an eight-year-old boy in San Jose, California. Under California law at the time, the two youths over age sixteen were tried in adult court and sentenced to life imprisonment without possibility of parole. Even though Martinez's sixteenth birthday was only three weeks away, his case was heard in juvenile court, where the maximum sentence confined him in a juvenile detention center until his twenty-fifth birthday, when he would be released. An outraged public quickly mobilized to lower to fourteen the age at which a child could be tried as an adult; since that time California has become a leading proponent of the movement to reform the juvenile justice system by trying youthful offenders in adult court.

In the mid 1990s, Princeton University researcher John DiIulio and U.S. representative Bill McCollum (R-FL) sparked public fears of a burgeoning crime wave perpetrated by sociopathic, violent youths DiIulio labeled "super-predators."[1] In response to this scare, to actual increases in juvenile crime, and to federal requirements for proof of reduced crime rates in order for local governments to qualify for block grant funding, all fifty states toughened policies toward juvenile crime. Central to most of these policies is a provision to try as adults juveniles who have committed certain felonies. On the surface, such a policy seems straightforward enough—try a juvenile in criminal court before a jury. In reality, the issue is more complex, with each state setting its own guidelines for circumstances under which juveniles will be transferred to adult criminal court and for how the juvenile will interface with the adult court, if at all. State laws differ not only in which of several processes they employ to transfer the juvenile to criminal court, but also in whether the juvenile remains within the adult criminal system or is transferred back to the juvenile system. Furthermore, the issue is complicated by differences in how the juvenile justice system and the adult criminal system in each state handle the various steps in the process from confinement, trial, sentencing, and incarceration.

Transfer options

With provisions to try juveniles as adults in place in all fifty states, states must provide the legal mechanism for transferring a juvenile to adult court. Generally speaking, for each case one of three mechanisms is used, and states may authorize the use of one or all. These mechanisms are judicial waiver, direct file (also called prosecutorial waiver or prosecutorial transfer), and statutory exclusion (also called mandatory transfer). Other transfer provisions exist in some states.

Under the judicial waiver provision, a judge from juvenile court examines the case and determines that the juvenile is unfit for juvenile court. The determination is made at a hearing and usually means the juvenile has failed to show benefit of previous attempts at rehabilitation, although seriousness of the offense, premeditation, level of education, previous criminal record, and the child's living environment may also be taken into account. Judicial waiver has been criticized as subjective and open to bias and racism, as Arianna Huffington notes in *Salon:* "According to data from the Los Angeles Probation Department, 95 percent of the cases in which young people were found 'unfit' for juvenile court and transferred to adult court involved non-white offenders."[2] Nevertheless, judicial waiver is the most frequently allowed option; all but three states have a judicial waiver provision.

The mechanism of prosecutorial transfer is gaining acceptance. In a 1995 report the U.S. General Accounting Office found that ten states provided for prosecutorial transfer; in 2001, the number had increased to thirteen. Huffington, writing about California's Gang Violence and Youth Crime Prevention Act, states, "In Florida, where a similar law was passed, prosecutors sent almost as many young offenders to the state's adult courts as judges did in all the other states combined—and 71 percent of them were for nonviolent crimes."[3] Prosecutorial transfer continues to be a significant option, controversial because it gives prosecutors power that up to this point belonged to judges.

Thirty-seven states had statutory exclusion provisions in 1995. In this third option, a state may pass a law that someone who commits certain types of felonies will automatically be tried in adult criminal court regardless of minor status. These felonies may include murder, rape, other violent crimes, and any crime committed with a weapon. Some states mandate transfer of any juvenile charged with any felony offense. Juveniles meeting certain age criteria or juveniles holding a certain previous record of offenses may also be excluded from juvenile court by statute.

Other new types of transfer have emerged since the mid-1980s. By October 2003, fourteen states provided so-called presumptive transfer of juveniles to adult court. By this mechanism, the juvenile, rather than the state, bears the burden of proof of appropriate jurisdiction. If some provision in a state's legal code—the severity of the crime, for example, or a previous record of delinquency or probation—triggers a transfer, the presumption is that the case belongs in adult court. At the hearing the juvenile must make an adequate argument to stay in the juvenile system; if not, the transfer must proceed.

In addition, multiple states have in place "once an adult, always an adult" or "once waivered, always waivered" legislation. In such states, once a juvenile has been tried in adult court, even if found not guilty, subsequently the juvenile will be tried as an adult, no matter what the crime. Conceivably, even shoplifting a CD could result in the juvenile perpetrator being tried as an adult. However, in 2001, twenty-six states had reverse-waiver provisions whereby a juvenile who had been tried as an adult could be referred back to juvenile court for subsequent offenses.

Philosophical differences

In addition to a confusing array of transfer options with various names in various states, the issue of whether to try a juvenile as an adult is further clouded by differences inherent in the juvenile justice and adult criminal justice systems. From the beginning, the juvenile court has been an entity separate from the adult criminal court with an entirely different philosophy. Historically, the juvenile justice system was conceived to protect children, who were construed to be victims of their upbringing. Focusing on the criminal, the point of juvenile justice has been to rehabilitate, not punish. To protect the privacy of juveniles, records of juvenile court proceedings and criminal histories have been closed, even to adult courts; and judges, in consultation with other social service professionals as opposed to juries, find juveniles delinquent, not guilty. Until recently, juveniles have served their sentences in facilities separate from adult facilities.

Adult criminal court, on the other hand, focuses on the crime; serves to punish, not to rehabilitate; and makes proceedings public. This approach presumes individual responsibility for one's actions that many people believe minors do not have. This approach also is the basis for differences in other key steps in the justice system between juveniles and adults—apprehension, sentencing, and incarceration, in particular.

When apprehended, a juvenile is held in a juvenile detention facility or more typically is released to parents, generally without bail. Once the determination is made to try a juvenile as an adult—which in the case of mandatory transfer is immediately—the juvenile may be held in adult jail, where conditions can be harsh if not brutal.

Sentencing practices

Another area of significant difference between juvenile and adult systems of justice is in sentencing practices. Juveniles charged with felonies are generally sentenced to locked juvenile facilities until the juvenile reaches the limit of the juvenile justice system's jurisdiction, ages ranging from eighteen to twenty-five. Attempts to rehabilitate the juvenile through education, counseling, anger management training, job preparation, restitution, or other rehabilitative measures are mandated as part of the sentence.

In adult criminal court a finding of guilty for juveniles tried as adults generally carries the commensurate adult penalty. Rehabilitation is not a goal, and even if some rehabilitative measures are available in the adult prisons, availability of slots is highly limited. Critics of adult sentencing charge that juveniles whose character is still not hardened and can be positively shaped will emerge from adult prison no better prepared to live productively outside than when he entered.

Sentencing practices differ widely from state to state. For example, in New Mexico, a juvenile court judge may issue an adult sentence even if jurisdiction over a juvenile has not been transferred, as long as the juvenile has been found nonresponsive to attempts to rehabilitate in juvenile facilities in the past. Some states, including Minnesota and Michigan, use blended sentences, whereby a juvenile serves the first part of the sentence in a juvenile facility but is transferred to an adult facility when the age limit of juvenile court jurisdiction is reached. In some cases, the sentence is reevaluated at this time; the adult prison portion of the sentence may be waived, and the juvenile may be released. A blended sentence can be issued by either a juvenile court or an adult court judge.

Problematic sentences

Mandatory sentencing, i.e., set by law according to the crime, has come under particular criticism when the offender is a minor. California, the second state to implement a so-called three-strikes law, has applied it broadly, requiring anyone convicted of three felonies to serve a twenty-five-year prison term. Because in California second- and third-strike convictions include nonviolent property damage over four hundred dollars and drug offenses, youth can quickly accrue felony offenses. Opponents of mandatory sentencing point to third-strike convictions, including the theft of a pair of shoes, breaking into a church for food where the homeless had been given food in the past, and the theft of twenty dollars' worth of instant coffee, as proof that the practice is unfair and ultimately a violation of the Eighth Amendment, which prohibits cruel and unusual punishment. Nathan Barakin, communications director for California's state attorney general in 2000, weighs this argument: "It's true that most three-strikes convictions are for nonviolent offenses, and there's plenty of room for legitimate debate about whether the net in California is too wide. But no one will argue with the fact that the law does incapacitate people who have serious or violent habitual criminal records."[4] In 2004 nearly half the states have three-strikes laws.

Finally, the adult penalty meted out to juveniles tried in adult court can include capital punishment. The United States is one of only four countries to sentence juveniles to death (Democratic Republic of Congo, Iran, and Pakistan are the others, according to Human Rights Watch). In 2000, twenty-three states allowed the death penalty for crimes committed under the age of eighteen; eighteen of these allowed the death penalty for crimes committed by sixteen-year-olds. In 1998, seventy inmates on death row had been sentenced as juveniles.

Incarceration effects

Critics of adult sentencing of juveniles charge that incarceration in a juvenile facility has a markedly better effect than incarceration in an adult prison. Historically, delinquent juveniles serve sentences in facilities expressly for juveniles—usually group homes, shelters, detention centers, or boot camps. As more juveniles have been tried and sentenced as adults, problems stemming from juveniles being housed with adults have emerged, including prisoner-on-prisoner brutality and increased recidivism resulting from a veritable crime school atmosphere. The latter caused Vincent Schiraldi, in writing for *Corrections Today*, to conclude, "Apparently, if a teen-ager is locked up with an adult offender, he or she gets more than just a cell mate, the teen gets a role model."[5] A number of states segregate juveniles and adults within the adult prison. Increasingly, judges take into account the availability of beds when they determine sentences for juveniles tried as adults and may go so far as to assign probation rather than to house a juvenile offender in an adult prison with adult prisoners.

Thus the issue of trying juveniles as adults involves a range of legal, ethical, developmental, emotional, and pragmatic issues. *At Issue: Should Juveniles Be Tried as Adults?* clarifies the debate by presenting authoritative, reasoned opinion on an issue that continues to engage legislators, educators, and the general public.

Notes

1. John J. DiIulio, "The Coming of the Super-Predators," *Weekly Standard*, November 27, 1995, p. 23.
2. Arianna Huffington, "Prop 21: Hard to Tell the Poison from the Cure," Arianna Online, February 28, 2000. www.ariannaonline.com.
3. Huffington, "Prop 21."
4. Tamar Lewin, "Study Finds Three-Strikes Measure in California Is Much Overrated," *New York Times*, August 23, 2001, p. A-12.
5. Vincent Schiraldi, "Lessons Can Be Learned," *Corrections Today*, June 2000, p. 24.

1

Trying Juveniles as Adults Is Unconstitutional

Mike Clary

Mike Clary is a freelance writer in Miami.

Legislation giving prosecutors the power to decide whether to try a juvenile as an adult is unconstitutional. It violates the equal protection clause in that prosecutors have no uniform standards to follow in making their decisions. Furthermore, the legislation violates the separation of powers clause: legislative powers are handed over to prosecutors. The decision of who is to be tried in adult court should be made by legislators, not members of the judicial system. While several high-profile cases have focused attention on Florida's system, the principle applies in all states that try juveniles as adults.

W hen it comes to kids and crime, Florida is known as the toughest state in the nation. More juveniles are prosecuted as adults here than in all other states combined. And several . . . high-profile cases involving accused child killers have showcased Florida's zero-tolerance reputation for the world.

But Frank P. Triola, a soft-spoken assistant Miami-Dade County public defender, says Florida's tough reputation is, at the same time, both undeserved and reprehensible. "We are ruining lives," says Triola, 39. "And the joke is that we're not protecting the public by sending kids to adult system where they get no supervision."

Mike Clary, "A Call for Tempering Zero-Tolerance," *Broward Daily Business Review*, vol. 43, November 18, 2002, p. A1. Copyright © 2002 by NLP IP Company—American Lawyer Media. Reproduced by permission.

Arbitrary, standardless discretion

In an effort to stem the tide of accused first-time juvenile offenders being tried as adults, Triola is challenging the constitutionality of a 1994 Florida law that grants county prosecutors the discretion to "direct file" felony juvenile cases into adult criminal court.

He's not attacking the provision allowing prosecutors to direct file [file charges with adult court], but rather subsection 1 of section 985.227, which gives them what Triola calls "arbitrary, standardless discretion to prosecute juveniles as adults . . . [in violation of] the separation of powers and Florida's nondelegation doctrine." The law also violates the equal protection clause of the state and federal constitution, he claims.

[On November 18, 2002,] Miami-Dade Circuit Judge Jerald Bagley [was] scheduled to consider Triola's challenge [in his ruling] on a motion to dismiss in the case of Jose Carlos Reyna. Reyna is a west Miami-Dade County high school student with no prior criminal record who was 16 when charged with burglary in March.

In his 22-page brief, Triola argues that the law permitting direct filing violates the Florida Constitution's separation of powers doctrine by granting legislative powers to prosecutors. He also claims that it breaches the equal protection provisions of both the state and federal constitutions. "Where juveniles get charged is a decision that should be debated and decided in the legislative hall in Tallahassee and not in the offices of prosecutors across the state," he wrote.

Triola's brief cites the U.S. Supreme Court's controversial ruling in *Bush v. Gore.* In addition, he cites a recent study, conducted for the Florida Legislature, which found that children sentenced under the adult system were more likely to commit subsequent crimes than those whose cases remained in the juvenile system.

The goal, says Triola, is to get the constitutionality of the direct file law before the 3rd District Court of Appeal and possibly the state Supreme Court. But first he needs a sympathetic circuit judge to rule in his favor.

So far he has made his case to four Miami-Dade judges, as motions to dismiss on behalf of four teenage clients charged with felonies and direct filed to adult court. Judges Cecilia Altonaga, David C. Miller and David H. Young all have denied the motion. Judge Bagley is the fourth judge to consider Triola's argument.

Miami-Dade assistant state attorney Joel D. Rosenblatt has countered with a 12-page brief bristling with citations to court rulings that have found that minors do not have an absolute right under the state constitution to be tried in juvenile court.

In an election year, when appearing soft on crime could be politically suicidal for judges and other elected officials, the assistant public defender's quest seems almost quixotic.

State Sen. Victor D. Crist, R-Tampa, chairman of the Senate's criminal justice committee, calls Triola's argument "ridiculous." He says Florida's system for handling juveniles "is better than most" states because a judge, not a prosecutor, makes the final decision on whether the defendant is sentenced as a child or an adult.

Most radical juvenile transfer law

A decade or so ago, Florida was considered a national leader in juvenile rehabilitation, with a host of treatment programs for young offenders. But the state changed its approach in the early 1990s in the wake of rising juvenile crime rates and several widely publicized murders of foreign tourists by juveniles.

In 1994, the Legislature passed the most radical juvenile transfer law in the country, giving prosecutors broad discretion to bypass the juvenile court and send teenagers as young as 14 directly to adult courts. Prior to that, juveniles could be prosecuted in adult court only after a juvenile judge decided to "waive" the youth to adult court, which is still required in many states.

Florida is one of 15 states in which prosecutors have the power to send juvenile defendants to adult court. Juvenile judges here also have the power to waive juveniles to the adult side.

Florida now allows prosecutors to transfer to adult court any 16- or 17-year-old charged with a felony, as well as 14- and 15-year-olds accused of more serious felonies. Transfers aren't reserved for murder and rape charges alone. The Broward County state attorney, for example, considers transfer for any weapons-related offense [including theft of a weapon], burglary, drug sales, or escape from a residential placement ordered by a juvenile judge.

In Miami-Dade County, Leon Botkin, chief of the state attorney's juvenile division, says he personally makes the decision on all juvenile transfers after looking at several factors— age, seriousness of the offense, prior record of the child, and whether or not any adult codefendants are involved.

In 1995, almost 7,000 Florida juveniles were direct filed to adult court, compared with a total of 9,700 juveniles sent to adult court via judicial waiver in all other states combined. Florida's rate of juvenile transfers has steadily declined since then, to 2,077 in 2000, according to the Children's Advocacy Center at Florida State University.

> **//** *Transfers aren't reserved for murder and rape charges alone. The Broward County state attorney, for example, considers transfer for any weapons-related offense [including theft of a weapon], burglary, drug sales, or escape from a residential placement.* **//**

But Florida also leads the nation in the number of children in adult prisons. In 2001, the state had 395 prisoners under 18 behind bars in adult prisons, according to the U.S. Department of Justice.

In Miami-Dade County, the number of juveniles direct filed into the adult system is actually decreasing, Botkin says. In 1995, for example, of the 20,727 juveniles cases involving felonies and misdemeanors, 1,464 cases, or 7 percent, were direct filed. Last year, arrests fell to 16,100, and direct files dropped to 778 cases, or 4.8 percent.

The downward trend continues this year, Botkin says. He believes that reflects a decline in violent crime as well as "somewhat more confidence in the juvenile system and a more aggressive attitude on the part of defense attorneys to keep cases in the juvenile division."

Wrongheaded approach to accused juvenile offenders

Despite these trends, Triola is convinced that the state's current approach to accused juvenile offenders—particularly those without prior criminal records—is wrongheaded. His boss, Miami-Dade County Public Defender Bennett H. Brummer, has freed up his assistant for a significant part of [2002] to try to change the law.

"Prosecutorial transfers to adult court costs taxpayers more in terms of reduced public safety and money for incarcerating youth who, according to studies sponsored by the U.S. Department of Justice, can turn their lives around if given the chance," Brummer says. "Transferred juveniles are typically given ineffective adult court sentences rather than the residential programming and intensive probation supervision available through the juvenile court."

Brummer adds that, "the studies show that juveniles sentenced to jail, prison or adult probation commit a higher number of new crimes than the comparable group who were sentenced to residential juvenile programs and the intensive probation supervision available in juvenile court."

Triola explains, "I wanted to work on this after seeing a lot of kids go downtown [to adult court] and have their lives destroyed. We don't protect the public. We just send out a convicted felon at 17, and then the next time they come back they could get 30 years. It's gone too far."

In recent years, Florida has been the scene of some of the highest-profile transfer cases in the nation, including that of Alex and Derek King, 12- and 13-year-old brothers accused of killing their father with a baseball bat; 12-year-old Lionel Tate, accused of killing a playmate with pro wrestling moves; and Nathaniel Brazill, a 13-year-old accused of fatally shooting his teacher.

> *We don't protect the public. We just send out a convicted felon at 17, and then the next time they come back they could get 30 years.*

While an Escambia Circuit Court judge recently threw out the King brothers' conviction and issued a highly unusual order to settle the case, both Tate and Brazill were convicted in South Florida and given long adult criminal sentences. [On December 10, 2003, the 4th District Court of Appeal in Florida ordered a new trial for Lionel Tate, reversing the first-degree murder conviction and life sentence.]

A team of prominent attorneys, led by Fort Lauderdale lawyer Richard Rosenbaum, has filed an appeal of Tate's conviction that includes an attack on the constitutionality of the direct file statute. "Prosecutors should not be able to arbitrarily go around and act like ministers of justice," Rosenbaum says.

The white King brothers' conviction prompted protests across the country, but no similar outcry was heard when Tate and Brazill, who are black, were convicted and sentenced. These cases and others have fueled the perception that juvenile transfer is a civil rights issue, because minority youth disproportionately receive transfers to the adult system compared with whites.

> *Prosecutors should not be able to arbitrarily go around and act like ministers of justice.*

Botkin says he would prefer in many cases to send juvenile offenders to good rehabilitation programs. But that's not always possible, he says, because many of these programs are "overloaded," with two- to three-month waiting lists. "There is no question we send people to adult court that in an ideal world we would like to see in juvenile programs," he says.

Legal and constitutional point of view

While Triola agrees that the quality and availability of juvenile programs is critical, he's attacking the transfer problem solely from a legal and constitutional point of view.

He argues that by allowing prosecutors "unbridled discretion to exclude all 16- and 17-year-olds accused of any felony from the juvenile system," the Legislature "has abdicated its responsibility" and violated the constitutional doctrine of separation of powers.

Triola contends that allowing various prosecutors in each of Florida's 67 counties to develop their own standards on direct files violates the equal protection provision of the U.S. Constitution. To back up that argument, Triola cites the Supreme Court's *Bush v. Gore* ruling, which arose out of the infamous vote-count meltdown in the November 2000 presidential election.

"Because Florida left local canvassing boards to develop their own standards, a 'dimpled chad' might be counted by one board and rejected by another," writes Triola, a cum laude graduate of the University of Miami law school who joined the public defender's office in 1991. "Florida's direct-file statute presents precisely the same problem."

Triola also argues that sending juveniles over to the adult system, whose orientation is punishment rather than rehabilitation, is counterproductive for society.

In his brief, he cites a study sponsored by the Florida Department of Juvenile Justice to support that assertion. Drawing on 475 paired criminal cases from six Florida circuits in 1995 and 1996, the study found that 50 percent of young offenders transferred to the adult system are back in trouble after their release at age 18, compared with 37 percent of those who have been through programs designed for juvenile delinquents.

In addition, the researchers found that young offenders in the adult system are more likely to commit more serious felonies after release than those treated in the juvenile system.

The authors, University of Florida researchers Lonn Lanza-Kaduce, Charles E. Frazier and Jodi Lane and Donna M. Bishop of Northeastern University in Boston, refer to earlier but less rigorous studies which reached similar conclusions. "Transfer is more likely to aggravate recidivism than to stem it," they concluded.

Triola is hopeful that Judge Bagley may find merit today in his argument on behalf of Jose Carlos Reyna, now 17. Reyna was one of five friends who last March drove to a house in southwest Miami-Dade County where one of his pals wanted to settle a beef with his girlfriend's brother.

> *This is a social policy decision . . . these decisions of who should go to adult court should be being made by our legislatures.*

Homeowner Maritza Mercado told Miami-Dade police that some of the teens forced their way into her home, and one threatened her with a metal pipe. Reyna did not enter the house or wield the pipe, according to the police. Nonetheless, the Miami-Dade state attorney's office charged Reyna as an adult, alleging he was a principal in the crime. If convicted, he could be sentenced to 15 years in prison.

Assistant state attorney Botkin says Reyna's case is not a typical direct-file case, and concedes that Reyna probably would not have been transferred to adult court had there not been an adult co-defendant charged in the same incident. Yet Botkin insist that Reyna will be well-served by the adult system. "He is facing serious, serious sanctions if he commits another crime," the prosecutor said.

Neither Triola nor Rosenblatt made oral arguments before Bagley. Instead, both sides agreed to submit a transcript of the arguments they made on June 27 before Judge Altonaga in a separate juvenile transfer case.

"This is a social policy decision . . . these decisions of who should go to adult court should be being made by our legislatures," Triola told Altonaga. "Florida as a state has gone way too far. And the whole country knows that; there [are] reports all over the news."

Rosenblatt argued that direct files made perfect sense in a system where prosecutors exercise discretion every day to make charging decisions. "Counsel just doesn't like the broad power that the Legislature has granted to the state attorney," Rosenblatt contended. "But the argument that counsel is making should be addressed to the Legislature."

Bagley declined to comment on the merits of the arguments or how he would rule. But he told the *Daily Business Review* that he understands the impetus for Triola's challenge.

In the early 1980s, "the juvenile system was broke," says Bagley, who served as a Miami-Dade assistant state attorney at that time. "Now the [juvenile] system is better at controlling juvenile offenders. And if you put these kids away [in the adult system], they are learning the trade of crime and becoming more hardened."

If Bagley rules against his motion, Triola says Reyna will be forced to choose between a trial and a prosecutor's plea bargain offer—two years of adult probation in exchange for a guilty plea. If Bagley rules in his favor, the state likely would appeal to the 3rd District Court of Appeal.

Whatever the outcome, Triola vows to continue challenging a law that he says purports to protect the community but fails to do so. He hopes that he'll find one sympathetic trial judge, and get the issue before the appellate courts, where a decision in his client's favor would have an effect well beyond Reyna's case.

"We have tried four judges and there are what, 20 in the felony division?" Triola says. "So I'm not going anywhere." [Florida law provides for prosecutorial direct file of juveniles to adult court as of this writing.]

2

Trying Juveniles as Adults Is Immoral

Terence T. Gorski

Terence T. Gorski is an Illinois-based consultant who has developed community-action teams for managing the problems of alcohol, drugs, violence, and crime.

Children should not be sentenced as adults for a number of reasons. The practice violates international treaties. It subjects youth to cruelty in prison, often resulting in severe emotional damage, permanent psychiatric symptoms, and suicide attempts. The historical perspective in the United States is that youth can be rehabilitated, and the juvenile justice system has been built around that principle. That system recognizes developmental immaturity in youth and the moral obligation to give kids a second chance.

Should children and adolescents who have not reached legal age be sentenced as adults when they commit serious crimes such as murder. It is my position that they should not. Here's why.

According to Amnesty International, a human rights watch dog organization, the United States is the only Western democracy that sends youthful offenders to adult court and sentences them to adult prisons. According to Amnesty International the imprisonment of youthful offenders in adult prisons violates United States international treaty obligations prohibiting cruel and inhumane treatment of children and adolescents.

Is this an unwarranted or extreme position to take? I don't believe that it is. Most youthful offenders will be physically and/or sexually assaulted within seventy-two hours of admission to adult correctional facilities. Such abuse will continue to occur on a regular basis for the duration of their incarceration. The effects of this abuse are horrific and include suicides, suicide attempts, severe personality damage, and the development of severe and permanent psychiatric symptoms. These effects make youthful offenders sentenced as adults more dangerous, not less. Our willingness to do this to our children sends a strong message that the level of moral development of elected officials, judges, prosecutors and the general public is rapidly and dangerously declining.

> *Our juvenile justice system is based upon the recognition that moral societies value their children and seek to help rather than hurt, treat rather than punish, and rehabilitate rather than destroy.*

We need to ask ourselves an important question:

> *Are we the kind of people who are capable of inflicting cruel and inhumane punishment upon our children and adolescents?*

As a nation, we answered that question decades ago with an emphatic no. At that time we recognized that most kids deserve a second chance and can turn their lives around with proper no-nonsense treatment in rehabilitation oriented juvenile correction centers. We backed up our answer by developing a juvenile justice system that protects kids from cruel and inhumane punishment while providing rehabilitation, and teaching the skills necessary to become a productive member of society.

We did all this because it's the right thing to do. We did it because to do less would have been beneath us as one of the most moral nations in the civilized world.

Three critical principles

We built our juvenile justice system around three critical principles:

1. It is wrong to hold children and adolescents who have not reached legal age to adult standards. They are developmentally immature and often unclear about the nature of right and wrong and without proper adult supervision can have problems with judgment and impulse control causing them to act out impulsively without forethought;
2. With appropriate treatment most children who commit crimes, even the most violent crimes, can be rehabilitated and become responsible adults; and
3. A moral society feels obligated to give kids a second chance whenever possible by having a Juvenile Justice System designed to help kids change rather than punish them for past offenses.

Our juvenile justice system is based upon the recognition that moral societies value their children and seek to help rather than hurt, treat rather than punish, and rehabilitate rather than destroy.

The problem with punishment and vengeance

Not all youthful offenders can be rehabilitated. Some pose a real and present danger and need to be segregated from society. The period of confinement, however, should be designed to give youthful offenders a chance to learn, grow, and change. If long-term protective segregation is required, it should be done in adolescent correctional facilities which protect the children from harm.

> *When people mature to higher levels of moral development they recognize the obligation to break the cycle of vengeance and retribution.*

It is important to remember that *punishment does not work.* The threat of punishment is an ineffective deterrent to crime, especially for children and adolescents. Punishment is a failed strategy for changing behavior, teaching new skills, or developing new and more positive attitudes and beliefs. The only justification for inflicting harsh punishment is to deliver vengeance in accord with the Old Testament standard of an eye-for-an-eye.

Loved ones of victims may feel justified in crying out for vengeance. The result is tragic. Vengeance does not relieve the grief and loss. It also instills a sense of inner conflict and guilt. On a deep level most human beings intuitively know that vengeance breeds more vengeance and violence breeds more violence. When people mature to higher levels of moral development they recognize the obligation to break the cycle of vengeance and retribution.

Both [Lionel Tate and Tiffany Eunick] are victims. One is a victim of lethal violence inflicted by a twelve year old playmate. The other is a victim of a legal system that is rapidly declining into Old Testament morality or retribution. Tiffany Eunick, age 6, was the victim of violence perpetrated by an unsupervised twelve year old, Lionel Tate. Lionel thought he was playing when he emulated the moves and tactics of the professional wrestlers who were his heroes and role models. He watched professional wrestling week after week. He witnessed hundreds if not thousands of savagely brutal acts perpetrated by professional wrestlers assuming the personas of theatrical psychopaths. He watched as they savagely body slammed, knee-dropped, and kicked each other.

Immorality of violence

In his immaturity, he couldn't see that it was all a show. He had inadequate adult supervision. There was no one to point out the dangerousness and immorality of the violent displays he was witnessing. There was no adult present to impress upon his immature mind the danger of using such savage tactics on others.

Lionel, an immature 12 year old, assumed he could do to other kids what these heroic wrestlers did to each other. He assumed the outcome would be the same—no one would really get hurt. Tragically, the showmanship of professional wrestlers can become lethal when inflicted by one child upon another. Thinking he was playing, Lionel body-slammed, head kicked, and knee dropped Tiffany. It was over quickly. Lionel was shocked and traumatized to see that he killed Tiffany.

Is Lionel a hopeless psychopath who should be locked away for the rest of his life? He doesn't appear to be. Will throwing away Lionel's life bring back Tiffany or soothe the grief of her parents and friends? Probably not. Will Lionel be helped to become a better person as a result of his life-long imprisonment? Definitely not. He will be physically and sexually abused and psychiatrically damaged in deep and profound ways by his prison experiences. There is a strong possibility he will attempt suicide to try and escape the torturous consequences of his imprisonment.

A moral imperative

So why are we as a nation allowing this to happen? Part of the reason is because our adolescent treatment professionals, the experts trained and educated to know better, are standing silently on the sidelines. The clinical professionals who are obligated to advocate for our youth and to protect our juvenile justice system from destruction have failed to act decisively and effectively. As a result the safety of all children is progressively going at risk.

How many children need to be tried, convicted, and imprisoned in adult facilities before it becomes wrong? How many children must be destroyed by a criminal justice system going out of control before we do something?

3

Sanctioning Youths as Adults Has Broad Public Support

Daniel P. Mears

Daniel P. Mears is a research associate with the Urban Institute in Washington, D.C. His evaluation research on issues of crime and justice has been widely published in a variety of journals.

The 1995 National Opinion Survey of Crime and Justice offers insight into which segments of the population most strongly support trying juveniles as adults. Analysis of the survey indicates that married people who hold a punitive, "tough-love" philosophy of punishment are the strongest supporters, especially regarding three categories of offenses: selling illegal drugs, committing property crime, and committing violent crime. Few if any connections can be made between race, household size, or conservative religious/political views and support for sanctioning youths as adults.

In recent years, getting tough with juvenile offenders has become a prominent focus of reforms and political campaigns. Central to these efforts has been the increased expansion of laws enabling youths to be transferred from juvenile to criminal court, especially for the commission of violent and drug offenses. This trend clearly runs counter to the *parens patriae* (state as parent) foundation of the juvenile court, in which rehabilitation and the "best interests" of the child were viewed as being of paramount importance. It also runs counter to public opinion in America, which generally holds that rehabilitation, particularly for juveniles, should be a central feature of sanctioning. Indeed, survey research consistently reveals considerable support among Americans for investing in nonpunitive, rehabilitative sanctioning, especially where youths are concerned. Given recent expansions in juvenile transfer laws, the question thus emerges as to the link between support for rehabilitative sanctioning and transfer of youths to adult court. The more general question is, Who supports sanctioning youths as adults and why?

Although substantial research has been conducted on public opinion and punishment, much of it remains primarily descriptive, prompting calls for more nuanced and theoretical analyses. The situation is particularly acute in the area of public attitudes about juvenile justice, especially given the transformation of the juvenile court in recent years to an increasingly criminal-like institution. Taking these observations as a point of departure, this article has the following three goals: (a) to focus attention on theorizing and explaining views toward sanctioning youths in adult courts, (b) to examine specific factors that to date have not been sufficiently addressed in the context of juvenile justice sanctioning, and (c) to investigate specific mechanisms, including marital status and political orientation, through which a rehabilitative philosophy of punishment may affect support for sanctioning youths as adults. The latter focus stems from what appears to be an emerging tension between conservative "tough love" approaches (e.g., George W. Bush's recent calls for "compassionate conservatism") and more liberal/ traditional rehabilitative emphases. In addition, the salience of "family politics" to policy formation suggests the increasing importance of examining marital status and political ideology in relation to policy issues, not the least including the criminalization of the juvenile court.

Theorizing possible linkages

Despite the considerable research focused on public attitudes toward juvenile justice, much of this research has focused primarily on use of the death penalty for youths, rehabilitative sanctioning, funding for treatment and vocational training, and fear of victimization. One notable exception is I.M. Schwartz et al.'s national study of demographic factors associated with support for trying juveniles in adult court and sentencing them to adult prisons. They found that the profile of those most likely to support sanctioning youths as adults for selling illicit drugs or committing property or violent crimes consisted primarily of males, persons approaching middle age, African American parents, and those who are fearful of being the victim of violent crime. However, they did not assess the role of philosophy of punishment or political or religious orientation or of factors such as income or marital status, each of which previous research suggests may be related to punitiveness. Moreover, contextual factors such as public disorder, urbanization, and crime rates, which research on the death penalty and fear of crime has highlighted as being of potential importance, remain largely unexamined in studies of support for sanctioning youths as adults.

> *Married people are more likely . . . to have, or to expect, children and, if so, to take a benign view of authority and a dim view of social disorder.*

Perhaps of more immediate importance than assessing whether such factors indeed are related to support for more punitive sanctioning of youths is the need to understand better why and how. In the context of juvenile justice, a focus on rehabilitative attitudes toward sanctioning is particularly warranted, given the foundation of the juvenile court on the idea of rehabilitation and the best interests of the child. One avenue by which to explore this relationship is to examine links between rehabilitative orientations and whether an individual is married. The latter distinction is important because marriage can be viewed as reflecting a commitment to mainstream conventional values, particularly those bearing on the notion of the sacredness of childhood. As M. Plissner has noted, "married people are more likely . . . to have, or to expect, children and, if so, to take a benign view of authority and a dim view of social disorder."

In theorizing possible linkages, two competing possibilities present themselves. On one hand, those who are married may adhere more strongly to conventional societal values which may contribute to their viewing youthful offenders as young

adults. In turn, this view may temper the influence of a rehabilitative philosophy of punishment and enhance a nonrehabilitative, more punitive orientation. On the other hand, those
who are married may be more likely to view youthful offenders as less culpable for their behavior, which may enhance the
influence of a rehabilitative philosophy of punishment while
diminishing that of a punitive orientation. Finally, insofar as
an interaction exists between sanctioning philosophy and marital status, the question emerges as to whether it can be explained by reference to political ideology. The latter clearly is
linked to sentencing policy formation generally as well as to
marital status not broadly but for specific political issues, thus
raising the possibility that sanctioning philosophy and marital
status may be linked to political orientation.

Data for the study

The data for this study came from the National Opinion Survey
of Crime and Justice (NOSCJ) ($N = 1,005$), conducted in 1995
and archived by the Inter-university Consortium for Political
and Social Research. Three dependent variables were examined:
Juveniles should be tried as adults if charged with (a) selling illegal drugs, (b) committing a property crime, or (c) committing
a violent crime. Each of these variables was coded 1 (*agree* or
strongly agree) or 0 (*neutral, disagree,* or *strongly disagree*) to focus
on the issue of who actively supports adult sanctioning of
youths. . . .

Three sets of independent variables were used in the analyses: sociodemographic, attitudinal, and contextual factors. Sociodemographic factors included age as well as age squared; race
(White versus non-White); annual household income (1 = less
than $15,000, 2 = $15,001 to 30,000, 3 = $30,001 to 60,000, 4
= greater than $60,000); education (1 = Grades 1 through 4, 2
= Grades 5 through 8, 3 = some high school, 4 = high school
graduate, 5 = some college, 6 = college graduate, 7 = graduate
work); marital status (1 = married, 0 = other); and number of
people in household. Although marital status can include a
wide range of possibilities (e.g., widowed, divorced, never married), the married/nonmarried distinction was most relevant
for the focus of this article. Unfortunately, the NOSCJ data do
not include information about children, thus vitiating the possibility of exploring the potential importance of this factor.

Attitudinal factors included political ideology, which was

coded dichotomously to emphasize conservative ideological orientations (1 = conservative, 0 = moderate or liberal), as well as views on parents having legal responsibility for their children's actions (1 = *strongly disagree*, 2 = *disagree*, 3 = *neither*, 4 = *agree*, 5 = *strongly agree*), religious denomination (1 = conservative Protestant, 0 = other), and rehabilitative philosophy of sanctioning juveniles (1 = rehabilitation, 0 = other). For religion, respondents were given denominational categories from which to choose; those who listed a specific denomination were coded as conservative Protestant if they described themselves as being Christian, evangelical, embracing the "full gospel," or as belonging to any of the following: Apostolic, Assembly of God, Baptist, Church of Christ, Church of the Nazarene, Faith United, Jehovah's Witness, Mormon, Pentecostal, Reformed Church, or Unity. For punishment philosophy, which will be central to the subsequent analyses, "other" included three options from which respondents could choose as representing the main purpose of punishing juveniles: deterrence, incapacitation, and retribution. The contrast thus was between rehabilitative and nonrehabilitative approaches to sanctioning.

> **❝** *Support for sanctioning youths as adults was greater among the married, and it was markedly lower among the better educated and adherents to a rehabilitative philosophy of punishment.* **❞**

Finally, contextual factors included a public disorder index . . . ranging from 0.00 (little or no disorder) to 4.00 (considerable disorder) and composed of views about eight items (trash and litter, neighborhood dogs running loose, graffiti, vacant houses and unkempt lots, unsupervised youths, noise, people drunk or high in public places, and abandoned cars and car parts); urbanization (1 = rural, 2 = small town, 3 = small city, 4 = suburb, and 5 = urban); and state-level juvenile (ages 10 to 17) property and violent crime rates (number of arrests per 100,000 persons ages 10 to 17). These rates were derived using data for 1994 or, when not available for this year, for the closest year for which the data were available; states for which other years were used included Delaware (1992), Illinois (1992), Kansas (1992), Massachusetts (1995), Montana (1992), Ohio

(1992), and South Dakota (1993). State . . . rates were used here because the juvenile sentencing laws asked about in the survey pertained to state law, and data availability and consistency tends to be greater for this unit of analysis; it also seems likely, especially given that local media coverage frequently focuses on state-level trends, that individuals consider state rather than local juvenile crime rates in forming opinions about juvenile crime and policy.

Given the considerable attention state legislatures have given to violent and drug offenses, the analyses center on three types of offenses (selling illegal drugs, property crime, and violent crime) rather than a composite measure of attitudes toward sanctioning youths as adults. . . .

Support for adult-like sanctioning of youth

Findings from this research parallel that of other research, albeit with notable exceptions due in part to different emphases, sources of data, and types of offenses examined. When the offense was property crime, slight evidence of a curvilinear relationship between age and support for sanctioning youths as adults emerged, with the greatest support among the youngest and oldest age groups. For this same offense, males were more likely than females to support more punitive sanctioning of youths. By contrast, an effect of income emerged only for youths tried for selling illegal drugs, with wealthier individuals more likely to support punitive sanctioning. Nonetheless, some general patterns consistently emerged across the three types of offenses examined in this study (selling illegal drugs, committing property crime, or committing violent crimes): Support for sanctioning youths as adults was greater among the married, and it was markedly lower among the better educated and adherents to a rehabilitative philosophy of punishment. In addition, few if any direct effects were evident for race, number of people in household, conservative political ideology, belief that parents should be legally responsible for their children's actions, conservative Protestantism, perception of public disorder, or living in an urbanized area or in a state with higher juvenile property and violent crime rates.

The fact that there is relatively widespread support for adult-like sanctioning of youths tried for selling illegal drugs or committing property or violent crimes and that, for the most part, this support cuts across many sociodemographic groups, contexts, and political ideologies, is striking. It does not belie the fact that widespread support also exists for rehabilitation, especially for youths. However, it does suggest the prevalence of a tough love approach to juvenile sanctioning that perhaps always has underlain the juvenile court but that today clearly is more pronounced and is, it appears, independent of juvenile crime rates. That certain factors, including marital status and philosophy of punishment, exert an influence that seemingly is independent of political ideology suggests also that views about punishment to some extent transcend political boundaries.

> *The prevalence of a tough love approach to juvenile sanctioning . . . is, it appears, independent of juvenile crime rates.*

To understand better such support, this study has called for increased research on and theorizing about public views toward juvenile sanctioning. Thus, a greater range of factors was examined than typically is the case, followed by an attempt to explicate the effect of punishment philosophy. The widespread support for "getting tough" with juvenile offenders suggested a need to focus more directly on populations in which markedly lower or higher levels of punitiveness and/or conservatism would be expected. Consequently, particular attention was given to sanctioning philosophy, marital status, and political orientation and interactions among these.

Interactive effects on "get tough" sanctioning

In examining potential interactive effects, several notable patterns arose. First, an interaction between philosophy of punishment and marital status was evident across offenses. Specifically, among those with a nonrehabilitative orientation, the married were considerably more likely than the nonmarried to support sanctioning youths as adults; by contrast, marital status exerted little differential influence among those with a rehabilitative orientation. Second, a three-way interaction between philosophy of punishment, marital status, and political ideology surfaced but only for the crime of selling illegal drugs. Specifically, among those holding political orientations and philosophies of punishment that were inconsistent (e.g., a conservative political orientation coupled with a rehabilitative philosophy), being married significantly increased punitiveness.

> *It is possible that people believe they are sentencing according to one principle (e.g., deterrence) and yet in fact are guided by another.*

The initial two-way interaction suggests that being married enhances a nonrehabilitative orientation, thus generating more support for tougher sanctioning of youths. This accords with the idea that those who are married have a greater stake in conventional mainstream societal values and therefore may be more likely to be threatened by affronts to society. The image thus is one of a group (i.e., those who are married and who adhere to punitive philosophies of punishment) that is especially fearful of crime and its potential consequences and, as a result, is more likely to view juveniles as young adults who warrant adult-like sanctioning.

An alternative explanation centers around the idea of a "halo effect." Specifically, couples who adhere to a nonrehabilitative sanctioning philosophy and who have or may have children may believe that their own progeny are (or would be) less criminal, whereas other children are predisposed to be more so. By contrast, among those with a rehabilitative orientation, whether married or not, there may be a greater inclination to believe that "kids are kids." Although this hypothesis was not directly tested here, the introduction of a family variable directly and in interaction with sanctioning philosophy yielded significant effects only when the crime involved a violent offense. This suggests that the interactive effect between sanctioning philosophy and being married may have less to do with the presence of children than it does with the state itself of being married.

Given that crime and social disorder have been prominent concerns among conservatives, the question is whether the observed interaction can be explained by reference to political ideology. The three-way interactive models provided tentative support for this possibility, but only for the offense of selling illegal drugs: Being married significantly increased the probability of supporting more punitive sanctioning of youthful drug dealers, but only among those adhering to inconsistent political and punishment orientations. One potential explanation for this finding, suggested by an anonymous reviewer, is that holding a consistent set of beliefs in essence may "trump" any effect of being married. By contrast, holding an inconsistent set of beliefs may lead those who are married to tend toward a more punitive punishment philosophy and, in turn, to support more punitive sanctioning of youths. Why? . . . Among the married, some couples may support select conservative causes even when they themselves are not Republicans or when they adopt liberal views on other issues. It may be, therefore, that in the absence of a broader platform of consistent beliefs, those who are married will tend toward more punitive sanctioning of youths, perhaps because juvenile offending is perceived to be a particular threat to marriage and family. Although this interpretation at present must remain speculation, it arguably is supported by the fact that this pattern obtains only when the offense involves the sale of illegal drugs, which is a crime that may be viewed as far more likely than most violent crime and far more serious than most property crime.

> ❝*Public opinion is neither monolithic nor simple.*❞

The interactive effects of sanctioning philosophy, marital status, and political ideology suggest the intriguing possibility that calls for tough love approaches to sanctioning—most recently and prominently the compassionate conservatism promoted by George W. Bush—have a basis not only in conservative politics but in broader social and philosophical trends in society. The fact that a three-way interaction emerged only for selling illegal drugs lends potential support to this view, especially given the long-standing concern in the United States about the role of drugs in undermining social order. More generally, the interactive effects suggest that our knowledge to date about how exactly different groups view sanctioning and its effect merits renewed attention. J.V. Roberts (1992) has noted that "in the context of sentencing purposes, it is possible that people believe they are sentencing according to one principle (e.g., deterrence) and yet in fact are guided by another." In this same vein, it is possible that among the married, there are radically divergent views of what tough love or compassionate conservatism means. For some, it could mean a pragmatic, nononsense type of rehabilitative sanctioning, whereas for others, it could mean retributive, incapacitative sanctioning. Until we understand better such possibilities, we will lack a sufficient basis for transcending simplified or nominally explanatory accounts of support for "get tough" sanctioning.

Widespread public support for sanctioning

Recent increases in more punitive, adult-like laws for juvenile sanctioning raise questions about the extent to which and why there is public support for such laws. Thus, this article has focused broadly on exploring previously identified factors, including those that have been less systematically examined, and, more specifically, on explicating the interactive role of sanctioning philosophy, marital status, and political orientation in support for sanctioning youths as adults. These issues are important because juvenile sanctioning has become a pressing social issue nationally. However, they also provide a unique opportunity to understand better the basis on which the juvenile court has been transformed from an informal, rehabilitative institution founded on the notion of *parens patriae* to a formal, punitive-based institution that increasingly resembles the criminal justice system.

Clearly, public support for sanctioning youths as adults is widespread and cuts across many sociodemographic groups and social settings. However, there are notable divergences, particularly with respect to sanctioning philosophy and marital status and to their interaction with political orientation. It is these interactions in particular that help elucidate the broad-based support for punitive sanctioning currently prevalent in U.S. society. Specifically, they suggest that this support draws its strength from overlapping and mutually reinforcing social roles and attitudes. Thus, for example, those who are married and adhere to punitive philosophies of sanctioning are considerably more likely than their nonmarried counterparts to support sanctioning youths as adults. However, the findings also suggest that being married is associated with greater support of punitive sanctioning of youthful drug offenders, but only among those adhering to inconsistent political and punishment orientations. Such examples suggest that tough love approaches to sanctioning may resonate with those sectors of the American public where sanctioning philosophy, marriage, political orientation, and fears about the consequences of particular types of offenses intersect.

Beyond these observations, there are critical issues that require closer scrutiny if we are to understand better who supports sanctioning youths as adults and, to the extent that they do, why. Such understanding is important not only for its own sake but to provide policy makers with insight into the kinds of policies that reflect public sentiment. Foremost among these issues is the understanding that public opinion is neither monolithic nor simple. As Roberts has written, "Public perceptions of offenders . . . are complex and far from unidimensional." As but one example, the support for trying juveniles in adult court for commission of select offenses should not be taken as support for adult sentencing. Indeed, Schwartz et al. found that although the "public prefers having juveniles accused of serious crimes (felonies) tried in adult criminal courts . . . [they do] not favor giving juveniles the same sentences as adults or sentencing them to adult prisons." Moreover and as noted earlier, research consistently shows that the public supports rehabilitative programming, especially of youths.

> *// Support for trying juveniles in adult court for commission of select offenses should not be taken as support for adult sentencing. //*

Echoing calls from others for closer attention to support for tougher sanctioning of juveniles, findings from this article suggest the need for considerably more attention to studying the relationship between philosophy of punishment and other factors. Marital status constitutes an especially neglected area of analysis, particularly in relation to political orientation and support for various public policies. For example, one avenue of research that needs to be better understood is the relationship between specific marital statuses, transitions into marriage, having children, and political ideology and how these bear on philosophy of punishment, broadly construed, as well as on support for tougher sanctioning of juveniles. More generally, researchers should consider carefully the precise mechanisms through which philosophies of punishment affect support for particular sanctioning options.

Additional attitudinal factors

In addition to increased attention to philosophies of punishment, there also is a need for considerably more attention to other factors and to developing theories that can anticipate or account for particular relationships. For example, previous research has emphasized the role of fear of crime and of having children, but there are many other situational and social contextual factors that remain to be examined closely, including the role of victimization of family or friends, views toward the potentially mitigating influence of a youth's history of abuse, media coverage of crime, age composition of a given area, unemployment rates, religious heterogeneity, and so forth. Among other things, such research will help clarify the extent to which attitudinal factors indeed are more associated with punitive sanctioning than are sociodemographic or social structural factors or the way in which these various factors are linked.

In short, there is much empirical and theoretical work to be done to further our understanding of public support for sanctioning youths as adults. Given the profound changes to the juvenile court in recent years, there is a compelling need for such work. Indeed, if the juvenile justice system is to develop on a more rational basis or at least is to reflect accurately public opinion, the complexity behind their views will require more realistic and nuanced accounts. On the 100th anniversary of the first juvenile court in the United States, it is none too soon to begin developing a sounder foundation for juvenile justice policy.

4

The Juvenile Justice System Is Too Lenient on Violent Offenders

Linda J. Collier

Linda J. Collier has served as guardian ad litem, *an advocate for children whose welfare is a matter of concern for the court, in the Philadelphia juvenile justice system. She is a lawyer and teaches a course on juvenile delinquency at Cabrini College in Radnor, Pennsylvania.*

Young offenders commit violent acts at increasingly young ages, and statistics show the numbers rising at alarming rates—a 60 percent increase in crimes committed by juveniles since 1964. For this reason an antiquated juvenile justice system needs revamping. Historically, the juvenile justice system was intended to protect children from society and save children gone astray. Today it continues to operate under the principle of what is best for the child. This system is inappropriate for violent children who commit adult crimes. Lowering the age at which juveniles can be prosecuted as adults is a step in the right direction, but the practice should be automatic and nationwide.

When prosecutor Brent Davis said he wasn't sure if he could charge 11-year-old Andrew Golden and 13-year-old Mitchell Johnson as adults after [the 1998] slaughter in Jonesboro, Ark., I cringed. But not for the reasons you might think.

I knew he was formulating a judgment based on laws that

Linda J. Collier, "Adult Crime, Adult Time; Outdated Juvenile Laws Thwart Justice," *Washington Post*, March 29, 1998, p. C1. Copyright © 1998 by The Washington Post Company/Washington Post Writers Group. Reproduced by permission of the author.

have not had a major overhaul for more than 100 years. I knew his hands were tied by the longstanding creed that juvenile offenders, generally defined as those under the age of 18, are to be treated rather than punished. I knew he would have to do legal cartwheels to get the case out of the juvenile system. But most of all, I cringed because today's juvenile suspects—even those who are accused of committing the most violent crimes—are still regarded by the law as children first and criminals second.

Increasingly, children commit violent and deadly crimes

As astonishing as the Jonesboro events were, this is hardly the first time that children with access to guns and other weapons have brought tragedy to a school. Only weeks before the Jonesboro shootings, three girls in Paducah, Ky., were killed in their school lobby when a 14-year-old classmate allegedly opened fire on them. Authorities said he had several guns with him, and the alleged murder weapon was one of seven stolen from a neighbor's garage. And the day after the Jonesboro shootings, a 14-year-old in Daly City, Calif., was charged as a juvenile after he allegedly fired at his middle-school principal with a semi-automatic handgun.

> *This system was developed with truants, vandals and petty thieves in mind. But this model is not appropriate for the violent juvenile offender of today.*

It's not a new or unusual phenomenon for children to commit violent crimes at younger and younger ages, but it often takes a shocking incident to draw our attention to a trend already in progress. According to the U.S. Department of Justice, crimes committed by juveniles have increased by 60 percent since 1984. Where juvenile delinquency was once limited to truancy or vandalism, juveniles now are more likely to be the perpetrators of serious and deadly crimes such as arson, aggravated assault, rape and murder. And these violent offenders increasingly include those as young as the Jonesboro suspects. Since 1965, the number of 12-year-olds arrested for violent crimes has doubled and the number of 13- and 14-year-olds has tripled, according to government statistics.

Those statistics are a major reason why we need to revamp our antiquated juvenile justice system. Nearly every state, including Arkansas, has laws that send most youthful violent offenders to the juvenile courts, where they can only be found "delinquent" and confined in a juvenile facility (typically not past age 21). In recent years, many states have enacted changes in their juvenile crime laws, and some have lowered the age at which a juvenile can be tried as an adult for certain violent crimes. Virginia, for example, has reduced its minimum age to 14, and suspects accused of murder and aggravated malicious wounding are automatically waived to adult court. Illinois is now sending some 13-year-olds to adult court after a hearing in juvenile court. In Kansas, a 1996 law allows juveniles as young as 10 to be prosecuted as adults in some cases. These are steps in the right direction, but too many states still treat violent offenders under 16 as juveniles who belong in the juvenile system.

My views are not those of a frustrated prosecutor. I have represented children as a court-appointed guardian ad litem, or temporary guardian, in the Philadelphia juvenile justice system. Loosely defined, a guardian ad litem is responsible for looking after the best interest of a neglected or rebellious child who has come into the juvenile courts. It is often a humbling experience as I try to help children whose lives have gone awry, sometimes because of circumstances beyond their control.

The juvenile system neither treats nor punishes effectively

My experience has made me believe that the system is doing a poor job at treatment as well as punishment. One of my "girls," a chronic truant, was a foster child who longed to be adopted. She often talked of how she wanted a pink room, a frilly bunk bed and sisters with whom she could share her dreams. She languished in foster care from ages 2 to 13 because her drug-ravaged mother would not relinquish her parental rights. Initially, the girl refused to tolerate the half-life that the state had maintained was in her best interest. But as it became clear that we would never convince her mother to give up her rights, the girl became a frequent runaway. Eventually she ended up pregnant, wandering from place to place and committing adult crimes to survive. No longer a child, not quite a woman, she is the kind of teenager offender for whom the juvenile system has little or nothing to offer.

A brief history: Proceedings in juvenile justice began in 1890 in Chicago, where the original mandate was to save wayward children and protect them from the ravages of society. The system called for children to be processed through an appendage of the family court. By design, juveniles were to be kept away from the court's criminal side, the district attorney and adult correctional institutions.

Typically, initial procedures are informal, non-threatening and not open to public scrutiny. A juvenile suspect is interviewed by an "intake" officer who determines the child's fate. The intake officer may issue a warning, lecture and release; he may detain the suspect; or, he may decide to file a petition, subjecting the child to juvenile "adjudication" proceedings. If the law allows, the intake officer may make a recommendation that the juvenile be transferred to adult criminal court.

> *If a juvenile is accused of murdering, raping or assaulting someone with a deadly weapon, the suspect should automatically be sent to adult criminal court. What's to ponder?*

An adjudication is similar to a hearing, rather than a trial, although the juvenile may be represented by counsel and a juvenile prosecutor will represent the interests of the community. It is important to note that throughout the proceedings, no matter which side of the fence the parties are on, the operating principle is that everyone is working in the best interests of the child. Juvenile court judges do not issue findings of guilt, but decide whether a child is delinquent. If delinquency is found, the judge must decide the child's fate. Should the child be sent back to the family—assuming there is one? Declare him or her "in need of supervision," which brings in the intense help of social services? Remove the child from the family and place him or her in foster care? Confine the child to a state institution for juvenile offenders?

This system was developed with truants, vandals and petty thieves in mind. But this model is not appropriate for the violent juvenile offender of today. Detaining a rapist or murderer in a juvenile facility until the age of 18 or 21 isn't even a slap on the hand. If a juvenile is accused of murdering, raping or assaulting someone with a deadly weapon, the suspect should automatically be sent to adult criminal court. What's to ponder?

A major overhaul of juvenile justice laws is needed

With violent crime becoming more prevalent among the junior set, it's a mystery why there hasn't been a major overhaul of juvenile justice laws long before now. Will the Jonesboro shootings be the incident that makes us take a hard look at the current system? When it became evident that the early release of Jesse Timmendequas—whose murder of 7-year-old Megan Kanka in New Jersey sparked national outrage—had caused unwarranted tragedy, legislative action was swift. Now New Jersey has Megan's Law, which requires the advance notification of a sexual predator's release into a neighborhood. Other states have followed suit.

It is unequivocally clear that the same type of mandate is needed to establish a uniform minimum age for trying juveniles as adults. As it stands now, there is no consistency in state laws governing waivers to adult court. One reason for this lack of uniformity is the absence of direction from the federal government or Congress. The Bureau of Justice Statistics reports that adjacent states such as New York and Pennsylvania respond differently to 16-year-old criminals, with New York tending to treat offenders of that age as adults and Pennsylvania handling them in the juvenile justice system.

Federal prosecution of juveniles is not totally unheard of, but it is uncommon. The Bureau of Justice Statistics estimates that during 1994, at least 65 juveniles were referred to the attorney general for transfer to adult status. In such cases, the U.S. attorney's office must certify a substantial federal interest in the case and show that one of the following is true: The state does not have jurisdiction; the state refuses to assume jurisdiction or the state does not have adequate services for juvenile offenders; the offense is a violent felony, drug trafficking or firearm offense as defined by the U.S. Code.

Exacting hurdles, but not insurmountable. In the Jonesboro case, prosecutor Davis has been exploring ways to enlist the federal court's jurisdiction. Whatever happens, federal prosecutions of young offenders are clearly not the long-term answer. The states must act. So as far as I can see, the next step is clear: Children who knowingly engage in adult conduct and adult crimes should automatically be subject to adult rules and adult prison time. [In a juvenile hearing open to the public, Golden and Johnson were given the maximum penalty, confinement in juvenile detention until age 21, with the possibility of early release.]

5

Juvenile Offenders Are Endangered in Adult Facilities

Brian Hansen

Brian Hansen, a writer in Boulder, Colorado, is a former CQ Researcher *staff writer.*

Most states house incarcerated juveniles with adults and have no separate programs for them. This situation causes serious problems for the youth, adult inmates, and prison staff inadequately trained to handle the mix. Youths are far more likely to commit suicide or be raped in adult prisons than in juvenile detention centers.

L ife quickly went downhill for 15-year-old Anthony Laster of West Palm Beach, Fla., after he grabbed $2 in lunch money from a classmate.

When word of the schoolyard incident reached local prosecutor Barry E. Krischer, he decided to charge Anthony as an adult—even though the youth was mentally disabled and communicated on the level of a 5-year-old.

The charges were strong-arm robbery and extortion, and under Florida's tough juvenile justice system Anthony faced the extraordinary prospect of life in an adult prison. Meanwhile, because his family could not afford his $500 bail, he spent four weeks in the county jail.

Soon after the CBS television show "60 Minutes II" took an interest in the case, the charges against Anthony were dropped. But Krischer's office said the media spotlight had nothing to do with the dismissal. The charges were dropped, according to a court brief, because Anthony's victim recanted his original statement that he had been threatened with physical violence.

Krischer was unapologetic, however, about bringing charges in the first place. "The state [draws] the line when there is a threat of physical violence," said Michael Edmondson, a spokesman for the state attorney's office. "The intent is to show [juveniles] there will be an absolute consequence to their actions."

What happened to Anthony had its roots in the drug-related juvenile crime wave of the late 1980s and the series of high-profile school shootings that began in the late 1990s. The crime wave prompted some experts to predict that a new breed of youthful "superpredators" had arrived on the national scene. In response, nearly every state passed laws making it easier for minors to be prosecuted and incarcerated as adults. . . .

Most states have made little effort to segregate juveniles and adults confined in state-run prisons, according to Dale Parent, a project director with Abt Associates, a research firm in Cambridge, Mass.

"The majority of states follow a practice of dispensing young inmates into the general prison population," said Parent, whose firm is conducting a long-term research study on juveniles housed in state prison systems. "They might not put a small, vulnerable adolescent in a cell with a sex offender, but other than that, they do not segregate the youth, and they have no separate programs for them."

Holding juveniles in adult facilities poses big problems for the nation's jails, says Stephen Ingley, executive director of the American Jail Association. "Juveniles are not adults, and they can't be treated like adults," he says.

> *I don't think the general public really knows what it wants from its criminal justice system, and in particular, how it wants to address the problem of youthful offenders in our society.*

On the other hand, Ingley says, sometimes adult incarceration is necessary. "What about the violent aggressive youthful offender?" he asks. "As much as I hate to say it, there are some very, very violent youths out there, and they are very difficult to house in [juvenile] institutions. What do you do with the 16-year-old who happens to be 6-foot 3-inches tall, and 230 pounds? What do you do with that 'youthful offender?'"

Ingley says a shortage of adequately trained correctional officers has made it very difficult for the nation's jails to properly and safely house youthful offenders. "We don't have enough people to manage the adult populations," he says. "There are still many states that [haven't] mandated training standards for dealing with youthful offenders, and there are some places that don't conduct any training whatsoever.

> *Kids put into adult prisons are 7.7 times more likely to commit suicide and five times more likely to be raped than those put into juvenile centers.*

"It's difficult from both an operational perspective and from a societal perspective," Ingley says. "I don't think the general public really knows what it wants from its criminal justice system, and in particular, how it wants to address the problem of youthful offenders in our society."

Many of Ingley's concerns are shared by James Turpin of the American Correctional Association, the nation's largest professional association for prison staff members.

"Inmates as young as 14 are not going to act out in the same way as 24-year-olds when they're told to do something," Turpin says. "The typical correctional officer isn't necessarily equipped or trained to deal with that kind of special population."

Turpin says the new juvenile justice laws have created a number of difficult "socialization" issues within the nation's prisons, resulting in youthful offenders being housed with people "old enough to be their fathers and sometimes their grandfathers." And that, he says, creates all kinds of problems.

"I've talked to some older inmates who talk about how cold some of these kids off the streets are, and how they're scared of them," Turpin says. "On the other hand, a lot of these youthful offenders are pretty vulnerable, because of their size and lack of maturity."

In Florida, according to the report unveiled at the National Juvenile Defender Summit, two-thirds of the 2,500 juveniles detained before their adult court trials were held in adult jails, and one-third of those were held in the general population.

Federal law requires that there be "sight and sound separation" between juveniles and adults housed in the same facility, though inadvertent or incidental contact is not prohibited. Moreover, the law does not apply to youths charged or convicted of adult felonies.

However, critics point out that kids put into adult prisons are 7.7 times more likely to commit suicide and five times more likely to be raped than those put into juvenile centers.

For example, 17-year-old Michael Myers was not segregated when Broward County (Fort Lauderdale, Fla.) Circuit Judge Mark Speiser sentenced him in 1997 to 18 years in an adult prison for sexual assault. Myers shared a cell with 20-year-old Chris Soule, who had an "extensive and violent" prison disciplinary history, according to prison records.

But Soule apparently did not want a cellmate. He reportedly told prison officials that he wanted protective custody, because his father was a police officer and he feared retribution from his fellow inmates. But prison officials refused to grant Soule's request, saying they needed specific proof that he had been threatened. So Soule made his own threat, penning a note that warned, "I will do my best to injure any roommate I may receive in the future."

Two weeks later, Myers was moved into Soule's cell. Two weeks after that, Myers was dead. Soule had choked him.

Michael Moore, secretary of the Florida Department of Corrections, downplayed the level of prison violence. "Incidents will occur in any prison system, but the number of serious incidents in the Florida system is extremely rare. Moore said in a letter to *The Miami Herald*. "No prison system can monitor the activity of every inmate every minute of the day."

"We're a criminal-justice agency; we're not a social services agency," adds George Hinchliffe, director of external and legislative affairs at the Florida Department of Juvenile Justice. "Our first responsibility is for the safety of the public."

6

Transferring Juveniles to Adult Court Does Not Deter Crime

Harry Shorstein, Donna Bishop,
Aaron Kupchik, and Howard Snyder

Harry Shorstein is a Florida state attorney responsible for a successful juvenile justice program combining prevention, punishment, and rehabilitation. His coauthors of the following report are Donna Bishop, a professor of criminal justice at Northeastern University in Boston, Massachusetts, specializing in juvenile justice and youth policy; Aaron Kupchik, a PhD candidate in the Department of Sociology at New York University; and Howard Snyder, director of systems research at the National Center for Juvenile Justice.

Several studies that examined the effects of transfer of juveniles to adult courts in New York, New Jersey, and Idaho conclude that transfer laws do not deter crime. Moreover, studies indicate that four assumptions legislators make—the juvenile justice system is unresponsive to public demands; judges hesitate to transfer juveniles; the waiver process is biased against prosecutors requesting transfer versus defense attorneys opposing it; and judges in criminal court are much tougher than judges in juvenile court—are inaccurate. It has also been shown that upon release, juveniles incarcerated in adult prison reoffend sooner and at a higher rate than offenders who stay in the juvenile system, making transfer laws more destructive than productive.

Harry Shorstein, Donna Bishop, Aaron Kupchik, and Howard Snyder, "Transfer—Implementation and Effectiveness," *Serious and Chronic Juvenile Offenders*, December 2000. Copyright © 2000 by the Institute on Criminal Justice, University of Minnesota Law School. Reproduced by permission.

Questions: What are the various states' experience with transfer laws? What is the impact of transfer on deterrence and recidivism? What is the impact of transfer on the juvenile and on the criminal justice system? How do juveniles fare in criminal court compared to adults? How do criminal court judges sentence juveniles compared to juvenile court judges?

> *Those juveniles who were incarcerated were more likely to re-offend than those who were on probation.*

Does transfer provide a better method of public safety? Is there a general or specific deterrent effect when the legislature adopts these types of measures? In addition, are there incapacitative benefits that accrue from transfer? While these are important policy questions, there are not a lot of studies analyzing these questions. Donna Bishop, Aaron Kupchik and Howard Snyder discussed a few of the studies that do exist.

General deterrent effect of transfer laws

Bishop outlined the findings of the following two studies on the general deterrent effect of transfer laws adopted in New York and Idaho.

• In 1978, New York lowered its age of criminal court jurisdiction over murderers to 13 years old, and for other offenses, like rape and robbery, to 14 years old. To examine whether there was a general deterrent effect from the change in the law, one study looked at juvenile crime rates from before and after the legislation was enacted, as well as the crime rates for a control group—older juveniles in the same jurisdiction who were defined and treated as adults, and younger juveniles in Philadelphia who were treated as juveniles. The study found that, although the change in the law was well publicized and well implemented, it had little general deterrent effect.

• In 1981, Idaho enacted a law mandating the transfer to adult court of certain individuals, as young as 14, who were charged with one of five serious crimes. Again, to examine whether there was a general deterrent effect from the change in the law, a study compared the juvenile crime rate for five years before and after the law was implemented, as well as the crime rates for the same age group in two neighboring states, Montana and Wyoming, both of which utilized judicial (discretionary) transfer. Not only did the study not find a general deterrent effect, it found that the arrest rate for the targeted offenses increased in Idaho while it decreased in the comparison states.

Specific deterrent effect of transfer laws

Bishop and Kupchik discussed the findings of the following studies that looked at the specific deterrent effect of transfer laws.

Original study by Jeffrey Fagan—juveniles arrested in 1981–1982.

Jeffrey Fagan looked at two groups of juveniles: New York offenders 15 and 16 years old who were charged with 1st or 2nd degree robbery or burglary; and New Jersey offenders of the same age charged with the same offenses. The juveniles in New York were automatically excluded from the juvenile court while the juveniles in New Jersey were handled in the juvenile court. The study looked at the demographics of the counties involved to make sure these juveniles were, in fact, similar—the only difference was the side of the Hudson River on which the juvenile lived.

Fagan picked 400 robbery offenders and 400 burglary offenders who were charged in 1981 and 1982—choosing equally between New York and New Jersey. He looked at the amount of time it took before re-arrest; the proportion of juveniles re-arrested; the proportion of juveniles incarcerated; and the frequency of re-arrest adjusted for time on the street.

Fagan found no significant difference between burglary offenders who were processed in adult court and those who were processed in juvenile court. There was a slight difference for robbery offenders—those transferred were more likely to be re-arrested and reincarcerated, and were more likely to re-offend sooner. Overall, those juveniles who were incarcerated were more likely to re-offend than those who were on probation, but those who were sentenced to either incarceration or probation by the criminal court were more likely to re-offend than those who were sentenced to incarceration or probation by the juvenile court.

Replicated study—juveniles arrested in 1992–1993.

Aaron Kupchik also explained a more recent study that has replicated and extended Fagan's earlier study.

The updated study used the same counties as the original and added one more in both New York and New Jersey. It also doubled the number of juveniles studied. Both the original and replicated studies looked at 15 and 16 year old juveniles, although the replicated study looked at females as well as males. The replicated study also added more variables, such as prior juvenile court record, concurrent offenses, pretrial detention, and warrant information.

The replicated study found that juveniles in New York who were processed in adult court were almost three times more likely to be incarcerated post-adjudication. Also, the estimated time served in New York was almost double that in New Jersey. Both states were more punitive with regard to juveniles with a prior record, but across the board New York was more punitive.

> *Juveniles in New York who were processed in adult court were almost three times more likely to be incarcerated post-adjudication.*

Overall, the study found that there is a punishment gap between juvenile and criminal court regarding conviction rate, rate of incarceration, and sentencing length. Waiver to juvenile court (transfer back), available for juveniles under 16 years old, was frequently used by the New York criminal court, but waiver up to criminal court was rarely used by the New Jersey juvenile court.

As for recidivism, however, the study was inconclusive. For example, more kids were rearrested for any offense in New Jersey, while more kids were re-arrested for violent offenses in New York. Those juveniles without prior records who were processed in juvenile court tended to recidivate less.

In conclusion, it appears from those two studies that deterrence is not generally achieved by laws which exclude certain offenders from juvenile court.

Florida study.

Bishop discussed the finding of a similar study being conducted in Florida, which began in 1994. As background, Florida has a broad direct file (prosecutorial waiver) statute, so most cases processed in adult court are transferred in that manner. Prosecutors can transfer any 16-year-old juvenile who has committed a felony offense, and any 16-year-old who has committed a misdemeanor offense if he or she has more than one previous felony offense. Prosecutors can also transfer juveniles who are 14 and 15 years old and who have significant prior felony records.

The study used an automated database to try to match a juvenile who was kept in juvenile court with one who was transferred to adult court. Offenders were matched by offense, the number of counts involved in the transfer charge, the most serious offense in the transfer charge, the number of prior juvenile system offenses, age, gender and race.

When looking at the juveniles in the short term, a greater number of the transferred offenders re-offended and offended more quickly. In the long term, both groups appeared to re-offend at the same rate although this outcome seems to have something to do with including property offenders in the analysis (property offenders seem to benefit when transferred). The rate of re-arrest continued to be higher, though, for the juveniles who were transferred. Also, the transferred juveniles continued to re-offend sooner.

Thus, it appears that transfer did not have a specific deterrent effect. Although there was an incapacitation in the short term when juveniles moved into the adult criminal system, the effect disappeared in the long-term when the juveniles were released and then re-offended sooner and at higher rates.

Validity of legislator assumptions regarding juvenile crime

Howard Snyder presented the findings of several studies that looked at the validity of legislator assumptions regarding juvenile crime and waiver laws.

Assumption #1. The juvenile justice system is not responsive to the demands of the public—juvenile court judges are just slapping offenders on the wrist.

The waiver rates in Pennsylvania, which had not changed its waiver law in a number of years, were analyzed in order to see if judges changed their behavior due to public demands. For the time period studied, Pennsylvania had one excluded offense; otherwise, judges had discretion regarding waiver.

From 1986 to 1994, the number of waived cases doubled. The probability of waiver in a delinquency case went from one in 128 in 1986, to one in 78 in 1994. In general, a lot more younger children were being waived as were children with fewer prior offenses. Overall, the study found that judges were not insulated from public pressure.

Assumption #2. Judges hesitate to transfer juveniles to adult court.

The waiver rates of two states with a long waiver history were analyzed to see how often judges waived juveniles when waiver was requested by the prosecutor.

South Carolina. About 80 percent of the requests by the prosecutor for transfer were supported by the judge and, in the vast majority of the remaining cases, the waiver request was withdrawn by the prosecutor, usually because of a plea bargain.

Utah. The percentage of waiver requests that were eventually granted was also about 80 percent.

> **❝** Deterrence is not generally achieved by laws which exclude certain offenders from juvenile court. **❞**

Assumption #3. The waiver process is biased in favor of keeping juveniles in the juvenile system.

The waiver rate in Arizona over two years was analyzed to determine if there is a bias in that state in favor of keeping juveniles in the juvenile court. In 1993, Arizona had a judicial waiver process which placed the burden on the prosecutor to make the case for waiver. In 1994, it adopted a presumptive waiver process, which placed the burden on the defense to make the case for keeping the juvenile in juvenile court. The study found that there was no change in the waiver rate—about two thousand cases were waived each year. Therefore, it did not appear that the waiver system in Arizona was biased in favor of keeping juveniles in the juvenile justice system.

Assumption #4. Criminal court judges are tougher on juvenile offenders than are juvenile court judges.

The incarceration rate in Pennsylvania was analyzed to determine if the adult court was tougher on juvenile offenders than the juvenile court. In 1996, Pennsylvania passed an offense exclusion law. As a result, more juveniles went directly to adult court and the waiver rate by juvenile court judges declined by about the same number of cases. So there was really no difference—the adult court incarcerated about the same number of juveniles that the juvenile court would have transferred to adult court. The only difference was that the cases in adult court were not heard nearly as fast as the cases in the juvenile court.

Questions and discussion

Many of the audience members questioned the effect of prosecutorial charging practices on the results reported by the various studies. In the Fagan study, the researchers tried to account for prosecutorial charging practices by asking the judges and the prosecutors about the various practices. Also, the charges were only added to the study once they were verified by a prosecutor—in other words, the charges at issue were not the initial charges filed at the time of arrest.

One audience member also questioned whether the robbery and burglary statutes at issue in the Fagan study were similar since, depending on the statute, the level of the crimes can be very different. Kupchik noted that the researchers paid careful attention to the statutes and that they were indeed very similar in nature.

In regard to the recidivism studies, one audience member expressed the opinion that recidivism rates may be higher for transferred juveniles because the judges are transferring the juveniles whom they believe are more likely to recidivate, based on the information presented. However, Bishop reminded the workshop participants that it is the prosecutor in Florida who makes most of the transfer decisions, and that decision is usually made within the first 24 hours. In order to more fully answer such questions, the researchers are going back into the case files to find out if the prosecutors had information available to them that somehow affected their decisions.

Finally, an audience member asked how "incarceration" was defined in the Fagan study. Kupchik admitted that defining incarceration is a bit tricky, and they did their best to define the term so as to accurately compare the New York and New Jersey incarceration rates.

7

Minority Youth Are Disproportionately Represented in Adult Court

Jolanta Juszkiewicz

Jolanta Juszkiewicz is deputy director for administration of the Pretrial Services Resource Center in Washington, D.C., and has been editor of Pretrial Reporter *since 1993. She is project director of the State Court Processing Statistics, a Bureau of Justice Statistics project that collects criminal case processing information in large urban courts.*

While variation exists across court jurisdictions, and sometimes minority youth receive more favorable treatment than whites, in general there is a high degree of disparity between the treatment of minority youth and whites. For example, in number of felony arrests, types of charges filed, transfer process, pretrial release and detention, place of pretrial detention, results of prosecution, and sentencing, whites generally receive less harsh treatment than minorities. Besides finding racial inequities, the high pretrial rate of release of juveniles, high nonconviction rates, and high probation rates all strongly suggest that juveniles are transferred to adult courts inappropriately.

[Since 1990] nearly every state has changed its laws to make it easier to prosecute juveniles as adults. Traditionally, since a separate court for young people was created in Chicago in

1899, juveniles who broke the law were brought before the juvenile court. In rare cases, judges decided which youth were so violent or such chronic offenders that they were "not amenable to treatment" in the juvenile court. In such cases the jurisdiction of the juvenile court was "waived" and the youth were transferred to adult criminal court. Some states had legislation that automatically excluded youth charged with the most serious offenses, notably murder, from juvenile court jurisdiction.

> *In 9 of the 10 jurisdictions, African-American youth were disproportionately charged in adult court.*

Recently, however, states throughout the country have passed a variety of measures to send more youth to criminal court. These measure include any or a combination of the following: lowering the age at which juveniles can be prosecuted as adults; greatly expanding the categories of crimes for which youth are automatically prosecuted in criminal court; giving prosecutors the exclusive authority to decide which juveniles are charged as adults; and limiting the discretion of judges to overturn decisions by prosecutors and law enforcement officials.

Minority youth experience cumulative disadvantage

This shift in policy has occurred at a time of growing awareness of and concern about disproportionate representation of minorities in both the adult and juvenile justice systems. Numerous reports, including two by the Building Blocks for Youth initiative, have shown that youth of color are over-represented in the populations held in detention facilities and transferred from juvenile to adult court. In the Building Blocks for Youth report, *And Justice For Some: Differential Treatment of Minority Youth in the Justice System,* the research demonstrates that minority youth experience a "cumulative disadvantage" as they move from arrest to referral on charges, to adjudication, to disposition or sentencing, and finally to incarceration.

Disproportionate representation is not the same thing as racial bias. Some argue that over-representation of minority youth in the justice system is simply a result of minority youth committing more crimes than White youth. Even when that is the case, a fair analysis, however, requires consideration of police practices such as targeting patrols in low-income neighborhoods, locations of offenses (on the street or in homes), differences in delinquent behavior by minority and White youth, differential reactions of crime victims to offenses committed by White or minority youth, and racial bias by decision makers in the system. As noted in *And Justice for Some*, a meta-analysis of studies on race and the juvenile justice system, two-thirds of the studies of disproportionate minority confinement showed negative "race effects" at one stage or another of the juvenile justice process.

This study, the first of its kind, takes an in-depth look at the prosecution of minority youth in criminal court. It is distinctive in several ways. First, it includes the full range of "transfer" mechanisms, e.g., judicial decisions, prosecutorial decisions, and legislative exclusions. Second, the study is broad-based, examining all the major decision points in criminal case processing, from arrest to final disposition. Third, there are a sufficient number of Latino youth to consider them separately in the analysis. Fourth, this is a multi-jurisdictional study of juvenile cases prosecuted in adult courts in 18 large urban counties across the country. Finally, the findings are based on data gathered specifically for this study and not from secondary sources.

> //*During the first six months of 1998, in the 18 jurisdictions in the study, the overwhelming majority (82%) of cases that were filed in adult courts involved minority youth.* //

While the study echoes some of the findings of earlier reports regarding over-representation and disparate treatment of minority youth, it also reveals disturbing aspects of the transfer process. In effect, in most cases, there is no longer an actual "transfer" process. In a marked departure from tradition, most determinations (85%) to prosecute juveniles as adults are not made by judges, but instead by prosecutors or legislatures. Moreover, although prosecution in criminal court is thought to be reserved for youth charged with the most serious offenses, this study indicates that many youth who are sent to the adult system have cases that are dismissed, resolved without conviction or transferred back to the juvenile justice system, scarcely justifying their prosecution in adult court, detention in adult jails, and subsequent incarceration in adult jails and prisons. Particular disparities in the prosecution of minority youth are also evident. Thus, this research raises serious questions about the fairness and appropriateness of prosecuting youth in the adult criminal justice system.

A. Sample

This study includes cases that involved a juvenile charged with at least one felony offense. All the cases that were filed between January 1, 1998 and June 30, 1998 in 18 criminal courts were tracked from the filing date to final adjudication (i.e., dismissal or sentencing) in adult court or until March 31,1999, whichever occurred first. The jurisdictions are:

> Jefferson County (Birmingham), AL
> Maricopa County (Phoenix), AZ
> Pima County (Tucson), AZ
> Los Angeles County (Los Angeles), CA
> Orange County (Santa Ana), CA
> Dade County (Miami), FL
> Hillsborough County (Tampa), FL
> Orange County (Orlando), FL
> Marion County (Indianapolis), IN
> Baltimore City, MD
> St. Louis County (St. Louis), MO
> Bronx County (Bronx), NY
> Kings County (Brooklyn), NY
> New York County (Manhattan), NY
> Queens County (Queens), NY
> Philadelphia County (Philadelphia), PA
> Harris County (Houston), TX
> Milwaukee County (Milwaukee), WI

There are 2,584 cases in the study. They represent 100% of the total number of cases involving White, African-American, and Latino youth that were filed in the criminal court involving juveniles in the 18 jurisdictions for the first six months of 1998.

The 18 jurisdictions selected for this study were drawn from those that participate in the State Court Processing Statistics (SCPS) project of the Bureau of Justice Statistics, U.S. Department of Justice. Conducted biennially since 1988, SCPS tracks for one year a sample of felony cases filed during one month in 40 jurisdictions representative of the 75 most populous jurisdictions in the country. The jurisdictions that had the highest numbers of juvenile felony charges filed in adult court during the 1996 series of SCPS (the last year for which data were available) were selected to participate in this study. This produced a sample of 18 jurisdictions, with the remainder having too few cases to warrant inclusion.

> **//** *Most determinations (85%) whether to charge a juvenile as an adult were not made by judges. This was even more true for African-American youth, 89% of whom were charged in adult court through direct file or statutory waiver.* **//**

B. Definitions

For the purposes of this report, these terms are defined as follows:

Youth or juvenile: An individual who has not reached the statutorily defined upper age for original juvenile court jurisdiction in the state in which he or she is charged, be that 15, 16, or 17.

Minority: An individual who is of a race other than White or who is of Latino ethnicity, regardless of race.

Disproportionate representation or over-representation: The proportion of a group with a specific characteristic that exceeds the proportion of that group in the population being considered. Thus, if Latino youth in a certain county make up 25% of arrests and 50% of youth tried as adults, that group's proportion of juveniles tried as adults would constitute disproportionate representation.

Disparity: Different treatment of individuals who are similarly situated or have common characteristics.

Felony: A crime punishable by more than a year imprisonment.

Violent offenses: Include murder, rape, robbery, assault, and other crimes against persons such as domestic violence and negligent homicide.

Property offenses: Include burglary, theft, motor vehicle theft, fraud, forgery, and other property crimes such as arson, damage to property, and buying or receiving stolen property.

Drug offenses: Include drug trafficking, drug sales and delivery, drug possession, and other drug offenses such as possession of drug paraphernalia.

Public order offenses: Include weapons, felony traffic, and other public order offenses such as gambling, prostitution, rioting, corruption or escape from custody.

Transfer back: The process, available in some states, in which a juvenile charged in criminal court by a prosecutor or automatically by statute may petition the court for transfer "back" to the juvenile court.

Detention or pretrial detention: Locked confinement in a juvenile detention facility or an adult jail while the case is pending.

Public defenders: Attorneys employed in government offices to represent youth in juvenile or adult court.

Private counsel: Attorneys retained and paid by juveniles and their families to provide representation.

Assigned counsel: Private attorneys chosen by judges and compensated from public funds to represent juveniles in particular cases. Assigned counsel are often utilized in jurisdictions where there is no existing or no full-time public defender program, or when there are multiple defendants charged in one case who require separate counsel.

Analyses

The analysis of the data entails making comparisons between minority and White youth across all jurisdictions (aggregate analysis) as well as jurisdiction-by-jurisdiction analysis. Aggregate analyses report overall or average findings. In some situations, the aggregate findings may mask significant differences among the 18 jurisdictions. Consequently, where appropriate, the study presents site-by-site findings in addition to the aggregate findings. Indeed, a number of the aggregate findings suggest that the transfer process is not working as expected, yet these findings may not be true for any particular jurisdiction in the study.

Several types of analyses are performed in this study. First, the study looks at over-representation. For example, is the percentage of African-American youth charged as adults higher than the percentage of African-American youth who were arrested for felony offenses? Second, the study looks at possible disparities among racial and ethnic groups, i.e., of youth charged in adult court for drug felonies, are minority youth treated more severely than White youth? Third, the study examines differences across groups by asking, within each racial/ethnic group, the percentage of the group charged with a certain category of crime (or released before trial, or convicted, or sentenced to incarceration, etc.), comparing the percentages across groups.

Finally, the study provides findings on the overall impact on youth of the transfer process, regardless of race, by examining whether and when youth are released on the charges (either with or without money bail), the amount of bail, and the percentage of youth ultimately convicted of the charges.

Study overview

The study found that minority youth, particularly African-American youth, were over-represented and received disparate treatment at several stages of the process. In some jurisdictions, African-American youth were over-represented in felony charges filed in adult court compared to their percentage in the felony arrest population, most evident in charges for drug and public order offenses. African-American youth were significantly less likely to be represented by private counsel, and youth represented by private counsel were less likely to be convicted of a felony and more likely to be transferred back to juvenile court. Of youth not convicted of their original charges, White youth were twice as likely as minority youth to have their charges reduced to a misdemeanor.

> *Nearly two-thirds of the detained juveniles in the sample were held in adult jails pending disposition of their cases. Of those, one-third were confined with the general population of adult inmates.*

African-American youth were more likely to be held pretrial in adult jails, while Latino youth were more likely to be held in juvenile facilities.

In other aspects of the process, minority youth received treatment comparable to or even more favorable than White youth. For example, of youth released on bail, the average amount of bail for African-American youth was significantly lower than for White youth, and the average bail for White youth was significantly lower than for Latino youth. Violent cases involving White youth took longer to adjudicate than those involving minority youth.

> *Of youth not convicted of their original charges, White youth were twice as likely as minority youth to have their charges reduced to a misdemeanor.*

A number of the findings raise significant concerns about the manner in which youth, regardless of race, are prosecuted in the adult criminal justice system. First, 85% of determinations of whether to charge a juvenile as an adult were not made by judges, but by prosecutors or by legislatures through statutory exclusions from juvenile court. Second, prosecution in adult court is expected to be reserved for youth charged with the most serious offenses. However, several of the findings in this report suggest that cases brought against youth prosecuted as adults were either not particularly serious or not very strong. For example, a substantial portion of those prosecuted as adults were charged with non-violent offenses, and many were not convicted or were transferred back to the juvenile court for disposition. If one of the main goals of these transfer laws was to adjudicate cases of children who commit severe offenses in the adult criminal justice system, this study suggests that this goal is not being achieved. The findings suggest that the adult criminal court is taking on numerous cases that should be prosecuted in the juvenile justice system. Furthermore, despite the fact that a great many youth had their cases dismissed, reduced to misdemeanors, or transferred, two-thirds of the youth who were detained pretrial were held in adults jails.

Major findings

A. Felony Arrests
    Arrest figures were available for 10 of the 18 jurisdictions and only for African-American youth. (Available figures combined White and Latino youth.)

- In 9 of the 10 jurisdictions, African-American youth were disproportionately charged in adult court. This means that the proportion of African-American youth whose felony cases were filed in the adult courts was higher than the proportion of African-American youth who were arrested for felony offenses.
- African-American youth were over-represented especially in drug and public order offense cases. Although African-American youth accounted for 64% of all juveniles arrested for felony drug offenses, they represented 76% of the drug offenses that were filed in adult court. Similarly, while African-American youth accounted for two-thirds (68%) of all youth arrested for public order offenses, they represented over three-fourths (76%) of all youth whose public order offenses were filed in adult court.
- In some jurisdictions, the disproportionate number of African-American youth whose cases were filed in adult court was dramatic. In Jefferson County, Alabama, for example, African-American youth accounted for approximately 3 out of 10 felony arrests, but represented 8 out of 10 felony cases filed in criminal court.

B. Charges Filed

- During the first six months of 1998, in the 18 jurisdictions in the study, the overwhelming majority (82%) of cases that were filed in adult courts involved minority youth. African-American males constituted over half (52%) of the entire sample.
- There were variations among the participating jurisdictions, with minority youth constituting 60%–100% of those youth prosecuted as adults. In one-third of the sites, minority youth represented 90% or more of the cases filed.
- In six of the sites African-American youth made up three-quarters of the entire sample. In five of the sites, Latino youth constituted 40% or more of the sample. There was only one site where White youth represented as many as 40% of the sample. Eight sites had less than 7% Latino representation in their sample, while in three sites Latino youth represented more than half of the sample.
- In all of the major categories of offenses charged—i.e., violent, property, drug, and public order—the highest percentage of cases involved African-American youth.
- Although African-American youth accounted for 57% of

all charges in the study, they comprised more than 85% of drug charges and 74% of public order charges.

- Drug cases were filed against African-American youth at five times the rate of White youth (17% vs. 3%) and three times the rate of Latino youth (5%). Twice as many African-American youth were charged with public order offenses (8%) as White youth (4%). Five percent of Latino youth were charged with public order offenses.

- Although the aggregate findings showed that minority youth were more likely to have charges for violent crimes than White youth, this analysis masked differences in individual sites. In half of the sites, White youth were more likely than minority youth to have violent cases filed in adult court.

Table 1: Percentage of African-American Youth Arrested for Felony Offenses and Charged with Felony Offenses in 10 Jurisdictions, 1998

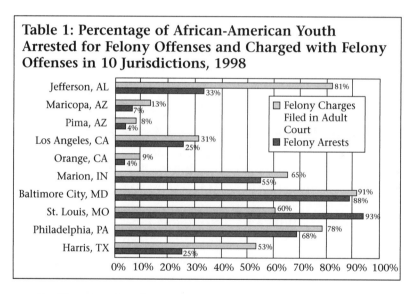

C. Charging Mechanism

- Most determinations (85%) whether to charge a juvenile as an adult were not made by judges. This was even more true for African-American youth, 89% of whom were charged in adult court through direct file or statutory waiver.

- More than 45% of cases resulted from direct filing by prosecutors.

- In almost 40% of the cases, the charges automatically excluded youth from juvenile court jurisdiction.

D. Pretrial Release and Detention

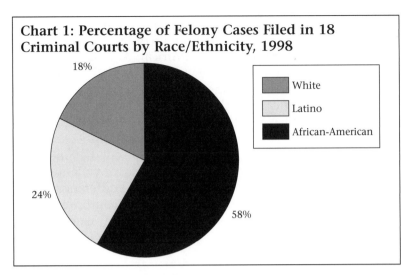

Chart 1: Percentage of Felony Cases Filed in 18 Criminal Courts by Race/Ethnicity, 1998

- The majority of youth in the sample, regardless of category of offense, were released before trial.
- There were differences in individual sites. While most sites released more juveniles than they detained, in three sites (Los Angeles and Orange Counties, California and Harris County, Texas) around 90% of their juveniles were detained pending trial.
- For violent, property, and public order offenses, there were virtually no differences in the release rates among the racial/ethnic groups. For youth charged with drug offenses,

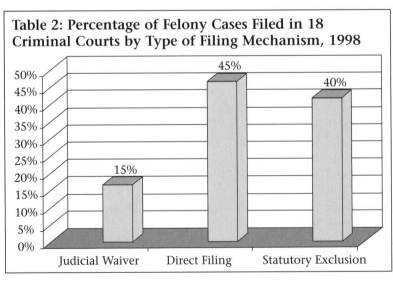

Table 2: Percentage of Felony Cases Filed in 18 Criminal Courts by Type of Filing Mechanism, 1998

however, a higher percentage of White youth (86%) were released pretrial than African-American youth (67%).

- For youth who were released on bail, the average bail amount was significantly lower for African-American youth ($8,761) than for White youth ($10,174) and Latino youth ($13,556).
- Significant numbers of youth were released on non-financial conditions: two-thirds of Latino youth, half of African-American youth, and 40% of White youth.
- Significant numbers of youth were not held longer than 24 hours: almost half of minority youth (46% African-American and 45% Latino) were released the same day they were charged, and more than half were released within 24 hours. Forty percent of white youth were released within 24 hours.

E. Place of Pretrial Detention

- Nearly two-thirds of the detained juveniles in the sample were held in adult jails pending disposition of their cases. Of those, one-third were confined with the general population of adult inmates.

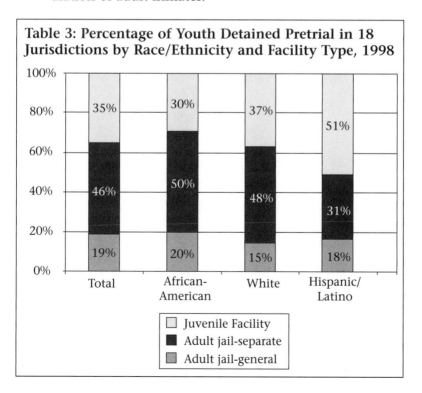

Table 3: Percentage of Youth Detained Pretrial in 18 Jurisdictions by Race/Ethnicity and Facility Type, 1998

• In four of the jurisdictions (Pima County, Arizona; Marion County, Indiana; St. Louis County, Missouri; and Harris County, Texas) all youth were held pretrial in adult jails. In the four New York sites, all juveniles were held in juvenile detention facilities. In the remaining sites, youth were held either in adult jails or juvenile facilities

Table 4: Percentage of Youth Detained Pretrial in 18 Jurisdictions by County and Type of Detention Facility, 1998

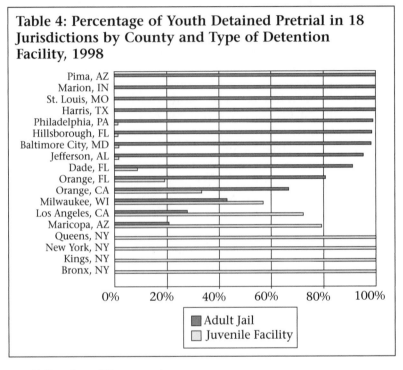

F. Results of Prosecution
• In nearly one-third of the 18 jurisdictions in the study, less than half of the youth were convicted.
• Overall, substantial numbers of youth were not convicted, and significantly fewer African-American youth were convicted than other youth. Forty-three percent of African-American youth were not convicted, as were 28% of Latino youth and 24% of White youth.
• African-American [youth] were much more likely to have their cases transferred back to juvenile court. The rate for such transfer back for African-American youth was nearly three times as high as for White youth (13% vs. 5%).
• Less than half (46%) of African-American youth prosecuted for a violent offense in adult court were convicted.

In fact, 20% of African-American youth prosecuted for violent offenses had their cases transferred back to juvenile court. Similarly, less than half (45%) of public order offenses against African-American youth resulted in conviction.

- For violent offenses, the median time frame from filing to adjudication was 126 days for White youth, compared to 88 days for African-American youth and 97 days for Latino youth.
- Of youth not convicted of their original charges, White youth were twice as likely as minority youth to have their charges reduced to a misdemeanor (13% of White youth vs. 6% of African-American youth and 5% Latino youth).

G. Attorney

- A majority of all three racial/ethnic groups were represented by public defenders. White youth were twice as likely as African-American youth to have retained private counsel (21% vs. 11%).
- Youth represented by private attorneys were less likely to be convicted and more likely to be transferred back to juvenile court, regardless of racial/ethnic group.

H. Sentences

- African-American (43%) and Latino (37%) youth were more likely than White youth (26%) to receive a sentence

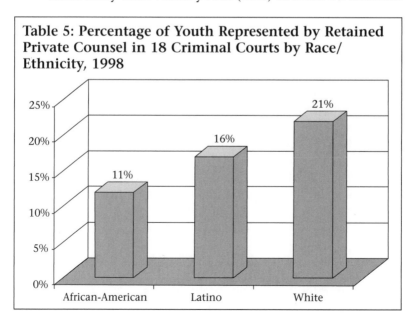

Table 5: Percentage of Youth Represented by Retained Private Counsel in 18 Criminal Courts by Race/Ethnicity, 1998

of incarceration (as opposed to a split sentence or probation). This held true when controlling for the adjudicated
offense. For example, of those convicted of a violent offense, 58% of African-American youth and 46% of Latino
youth received a sentence of incarceration, compared to
34% of White youth.

- Of those sentenced to prison, African-American youth in
  almost all offense categories had longer sentences than
  White or Latino youth.
- For those convicted of drug offenses, a lower percentage of
  African-American youth (37%) received probation than
  White youth (44%) or Latino youth (53%).

Serious concerns about fairness

Like the earlier reports by the Building Blocks for Youth initiative, this research raises serious concerns about the fairness of
the justice system. The data indicate that minority youth, particularly African-American youth, receive disparate treatment
at several points in the process. On the other hand, the data
demonstrate that the system is not monolithic, and minority
youth actually receive more favorable treatment (or treatment
that seems more favorable) in some circumstances. One value
of this research is that it allows a more in-depth examination
of these issues. In this study, however, it was impossible to explore in detail the reasons why these disparities exist. Consequently, there is a strong need for more comprehensive research in this area. One partial explanation for some disparity
is that White youth were twice as likely as African-American
youth to be represented by private counsel who are [not] bur-
dened by the high caseloads that public defenders carry.

Perhaps the most significant contribution of this research is
the spotlight it throws on those aspects of the justice system
that appear to work contrary to traditional reasons for prosecution of youth in adult court. The decision to prosecute a juvenile as an adult has momentous consequences for the individual involved. This study found that nearly two-thirds of the
juveniles detained pretrial were held in adult jails pending disposition of their cases. Of those, one-third were confined with
the general adult inmate population. Yet, the overall high pretrial release rates (often with no bail required), high nonconviction rates, and high probation rates suggest that the
cases filed in adult court in many instances may not be suffi-

ciently serious or strong. Since most states have committed themselves to increased prosecution of juveniles in adult court, this is clearly an area that requires additional research, policy review, and new legislation to ensure that young people are not unnecessarily and inappropriately swept up into the adult criminal justice system.

8

Severe Measures Are Necessary to Protect Citizens from Juvenile Criminals

John Ashcroft

John Ashcroft, a Republican senator from Missouri from 1994 to 2000, was appointed U.S. attorney general in 2001.

Government's primary responsibility is to keep its citizenry safe. Yet, as America's violent criminals are increasingly juveniles, the federal government has failed in its measures to reform them. It is time to hold juveniles accountable with tough measures. Provisions for trying and sentencing juveniles as adults will emphasize that committing adult crimes has adult consequences.

M r. President, the face of crime in America is indeed changing. Throughout our history, one thing has been clear: government's first responsibility is to keep the citizenry safe. John Jay wrote in The Federalist, No. 3, "Among the many objects to which a wise and free people find it necessary to direct their attention, that of providing for their safety seems to be first."

The murderers, robbers, rapists, and drug dealers of yesteryear were typically adults. Now they are typically juveniles. As the age of these criminal predators becomes younger and younger with each passing year, so does the age of their victims. [In 1997,] 12-year-old Darryl Dayan Hall was abducted at

John Ashcroft, address to the U.S. Senate, Washington, DC, January 21, 1997.

gunpoint from the Southeast Washington area by three teen-agers of a gang known as the Simple City Crew. This is the same gang that opened gunfire at a crowded community swimming pool in June 1993, wounding six children. [Four days later] po-lice found Darryl's frozen body. He had been shot once in the back of the head and at least once in the body.

> **"** *The murders, robbers, rapists, and drug dealers of yesteryear were typically adults. Now they are typically juveniles.* **"**

The three teenagers who are now charged with Darryl's murder have had numerous prior brushes with the law. One of Darryl's assailants was charged as a juvenile with possession of PCP in 1995 and then was released—as is too often the case—promising not to run afoul of the law again. Another of Dar-ryl's assailants was, and is, on probation following his juvenile conviction last spring for possession of PCP with intent to dis-tribute. Darryl's third assailant was charged as a juvenile just last month with carrying a deadly weapon.

The failure of the federal government

Mr. President, from 1984 to 1994, the number of juveniles mur-dered in this country increased 82 percent. In 1994, one of every five juveniles murdered was killed by another juvenile. The rate at which juveniles 14 to 17 years old were arrested for murder grew by 22 percent from 1990 to 1994 and the problem is going to get worse, much worse.

Congress over the last three decades has established 131 separate Federal programs—administered by 16 different de-partments and agencies—to serve delinquent and at-risk youth, according to a report issued by [the Government Accountabil-ity Office in] March [1996]. Conservative estimates of Federal appropriations used for these at-risk and delinquent youth pro-grams was more than $4 billion in fiscal year 1995.

Despite this ongoing massive expenditure, the Federal Gov-ernment has failed to meet its responsibility of providing pub-lic safety in this arena because it has not focused on holding ju-veniles accountable for their violent crimes. We now have a new category of offenders that requires a different, tougher approach. In short, we have criminals in our midst—young criminals—not juvenile pranksters and truants.

The juvenile offenders of today will become the career criminals of tomorrow, if government continues to fail to recognize that America has an acute social illness that cannot be cured solely with money spent on social programs. [The Violent and Repeat Offender Act of 1997[1]] takes a common sense approach in dealing with the current epidemic of juvenile violence. It would help States make urban, suburban, and rural communities safe once again.

Provisions of the Violent and Repeat Offender Act of 1997

The bill would provide $2.5 billion over 5 years in new incentive grants for States to enact accountability-based reforms in their juvenile justice systems. This legislation would authorize funding for various programs, including efforts aimed at trying our most violent juveniles as adults; establishing the ability of States to collect juvenile criminal records, fingerprints, and photographs, and to share such criminal histories and information within a State, with other States, and with the Federal Government; and establishing Serious Habitual Offender Comprehensive Action Program (SHOCAP). Religious organizations would also be permitted to participate in the rehabilitative programs included in the bill.

> *Today we are living with a juvenile justice system that was created around the time of the silent film.*

Mr. President, serious, violent, and repeat juvenile offenders must be held responsible for their crimes. Today we are living with a juvenile justice system that was created around the time of the silent film. We are living with a juvenile justice system that reprimands the crime victim for being at the wrong

---

1. The Violent and Repeat Offender Act of 1997 did not pass the Judiciary Committee.

place at the wrong time, and then turns around and hugs the juvenile terrorist, whispering ever so softly into his ear, "Don't worry, the State will cure you."

The juvenile justice system's primary goal today is to treat and rehabilitate the juvenile offender. Such a system can handle runaways, truants, and other status offenders; but it is ill-equipped to deal with those who commit serious and violent juvenile crimes repeatedly.

The criminal justice system can emphasize to adult criminals that acts have real consequences. The purpose of the criminal justice system is to punish, that is, to hold defendants accountable.

This legislation would provide financial assistance to States to help them reform their juvenile justice system to get the message to juveniles that their acts have real consequences to them as well. States will be eligible to receive Federal funds to help provide for the adult prosecution—as a matter of law or prosecutorial discretion—of juveniles 14 or older who commit violent crimes such as murder, forcible rape, armed robbery, and assault with a deadly weapon or offenses involving controlled substances or involving the possession of a firearm or a destructive device.

An effective tool

Mr. President, punishing dangerous juveniles as adults is an effective tool in fighting violent juvenile crime. For example, in Jacksonville, FL, State Attorney Harry Shorstein instituted a program to prosecute and incarcerate such offenders in 1992. Two years later, the number of juveniles arrested in the city dropped from 7,184 to 5,475. While juvenile arrests increased for most of the Nation, Jacksonville's arrest rate actually decreased by 30 percent. . . .

Mr. President, for purposes of adult sentencing, adult courts need to know that convicted felons have a history of criminal behavior. According to the 1991 Survey of Inmates in State Correctional Facilities, nearly 40 percent of prison inmates also had prior criminal records as juveniles. That is approximately 4 in 10 prison inmates. The proposed legislation would allow adult courts to have access to juvenile records so that criminals could no longer masquerade as neophytes before the adult criminal justice system. . . .

Mr. President, reforms are also necessary at the Federal level as well. [The Violent and Repeat Offender Act of 1997] would make it easier for Federal prosecutors to try juveniles as adults. Under the bill, U.S. attorneys would have discretion to decide whether to try as adults juveniles 14 years or older without having to go through the Attorney General's office in Washington.

Federal juvenile court proceedings would be opened to the general public. When imposing a sentence, the district court would also be allowed to consider a juvenile's entire criminal record under the bill. In any case in which a juvenile is tried as an adult, access to the record of that offense would be made available to law enforcement authorities and others in the same manner that adult criminal records are publicly available. . . .

We as a nation and a government must challenge this culture of violence and restore the culture of personal responsibility and accountability. It is high time to consider hard-headed and sensible juvenile justice policies. Where possible we must give second chances. Where necessary we must punish severely. This is a first step to restore justice to a nation that has grown weary of injustice.

In sum, this legislation would send a clear, cogent, and convincing message to violent juveniles: "Serious acts have serious consequences."

9

Juvenile Offenders Have Been Unfairly Demonized

Linda S. Beres and Thomas D. Griffith

Linda S. Beres is a professor of law at Loyola Law School in Los Angeles. Thomas D. Griffith is John B. Milliken Professor of Taxation, University of Southern California Law School.

Demonizing youth while framing crime control as a "war" encourages a climate of police brutality and draconian anticrime measures. One such measure is the proposal to turn over to prosecutors the decision whether to try fourteen-year-olds as adults. Furthermore, detailed descriptions of young men of color, especially those suspected of gang membership, may be entered into a secret database not open to the public, leaving the youths vulnerable to police harassment. Ultimately, reliance on extreme measures such as these discourages less punitive, often more cost-effective methods of crime control.

Youth in general, and young minority males in particular, often are demonized by legislators, the media, scholars, and the public at large. These attacks reinforce stereotypes and place a particularly heavy burden on young Black and Latino males. Negative images of youth also may inhibit the adoption of the most effective programs to reduce crime, especially in disadvantaged inner-city neighborhoods.

Viewing young minority males as the enemy fosters illegal police conduct like that exhibited by the Rampart CRASH unit. Indeed, the name itself, *Community Response to Street Hoodlums*,

Linda S. Beres and Thomas D. Griffith, "Demonizing Youth," *Loyola of Los Angeles Law Review*, vol. 34, January 2001, pp. 747–67. Copyright © 2001 by *Loyola of Los Angeles Law Review*. Reproduced by permission.

evokes images of incorrigible offenders for whom rehabilitation programs are fruitless. Conceptualizing the crime-control mission in military terms—"War on Drugs" and "War on Gangs"—can encourage an "ends justifies the means" attitude. The resulting police conduct can vary from the oft-reported false testifying of officers regarding the circumstances surrounding a stop or search, to the more extreme case of shooting and then framing an innocent man. This same attitude can lead prosecutors and judges to accept questionable police testimony. In addition, it can lead voters to pass draconian anti-crime measures directed against young offenders, such as Proposition 21.

> *// Conceptualizing the crime-control mission in military terms—'War on Drugs' and 'War on Gangs'—can encourage an 'ends justifies the means' attitude. //*

Although titled the "Gang Violence and Juvenile Crime Prevention Act of 1998," Prop. 21 was approved by the voters in an initiative referendum on March 7, 2000. Prop. 21 provided several "get tough" measures for participants in gang-related activities. It also transferred from judges to prosecutors the power to decide whether offenders as young as fourteen would be tried as adults or as juveniles for certain serious crimes. An analysis of Prop. 21 is beyond the scope of this article. It is revealing, however, to examine its "Finding and Declarations." These include:

- "While overall crime is declining, juvenile crime has become a larger and more ominous threat."
- "[F]rom 1983 to 1992 . . . murders committed by juveniles more than doubled."
- "Criminal street gangs have become more violent, bolder, and better organized in recent years."
- "Vigorous enforcement and the adoption of more meaningful criminal sanctions, including [Three Strikes] has resulted in a substantial and consistent four year decline in overall crime. Violent juvenile crime has proven most resistant to this positive trend."
- "Gang-related crimes pose a unique threat to the public because of gang members' organization and solidarity."

• "Dramatic changes are needed in the way we treat juvenile criminals, criminal street gangs, and the confidentiality of the juvenile records of violent offenders if we are to avoid the predicted, unprecedented surge in juvenile and gang violence."

Draconian measures based on false assumptions

In short, the backers of Prop. 21 argue that tougher penalties for youth crime are needed because violent crime by youths, and especially by youths in gangs, is increasing now and will likely increase even more rapidly in the near future. Prop. 21's "finding" of a "predicted, unprecedented surge in juvenile and gang violence" is based on two factual assumptions:

1. The number of juveniles in the "crime-prone ages between 12 and 17" is going to increase significantly in the near future.
2. These youths will be much more dangerous than those of prior generations.

It is far from clear, however, that the ages 12 to 17 are the "crime-prone ages" or that the coming youth cohort is more dangerous than prior cohorts.

Are serious violent crimes most likely to be committed by individuals between the ages of 12 and 17? Consider Figure 1,

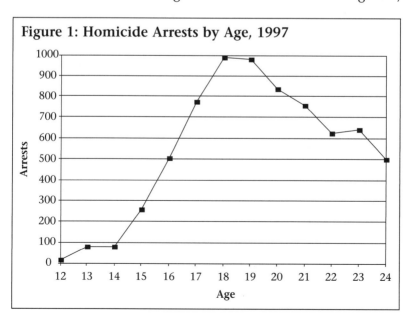

Figure 1: Homicide Arrests by Age, 1997

which shows the number of homicide arrests by age in the United States in 1997.

Homicide arrest rates are highest from age 17 to 21 with the peaks occurring at ages 18 and 19. Homicides by youths under the age of 16 are relatively rare. A similar pattern occurs for violent crime generally, as shown in Figure 2.[1] Arrest statistics, moreover, overstate the extent of youth crime because teenagers tend to commit crimes in groups.

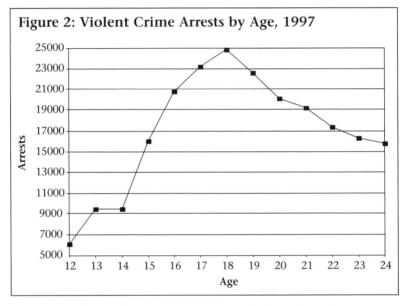

Figure 2: Violent Crime Arrests by Age, 1997

Arrests for violent crimes peak slightly earlier than arrests for homicide, largely due to arrests of youths for aggravated assault. Violent crime arrests are highest from age 17 to 19 with the peak occurring at age 18.

Contrary to the claims of Prop. 21, the most crime prone ages are 17 to 21, not ages 12 to 17. Nevertheless, it is true that 17-year-old youths and, to a lesser extent, 16-year-old youths do commit crimes at a fairly high rate, similar to that of individuals in their early 20s. But the backers of Prop. 21 mislead the public when they lump the crime rates for 16 and 17-year-olds together with the much lower crime rates for 12 to 14-year-olds.

1. Violent crimes are murder and nonnegligent manslaughter, forcible rape, robbery, and aggravated assault. Violent crime statistics are dominated by aggravated assault because there are far more arrests for this offense than for all other violent crimes combined.

Legislation to require trying youths as adults

Perhaps more frightening than the projected growth in the number of young teenagers is the prediction that these teenagers will be much more likely to commit serious violent crime than teenagers in the past. The most prominent advocate of this claim is John J. DiIulio, Jr. [who has recanted the most extreme predictions made in his 1995 book *The Coming of the Super-Predators*]. As youth crime rose in the late 1980s and early 1990s, DiIulio's warning of the emergence of a new, more dangerous type of youthful offender was widely reported in the popular press. DiIulio continued to sound the alarm even as violent youth crime was beginning to decline in the mid-1990s.

DiIulio coined the lurid phrase "super-predators" to describe this new breed of juvenile offenders. The image evoked was one of individuals devoid of humanity: "[A] few years ago, I forswore research inside juvenile lock-ups. The buzz of impulsive violence, the vacant stares and smiles, and the remorseless eyes were at once too frightening and too depressing (my God, these are children!) for me to pretend to 'study' them."

> *The backers of Prop. 21 mislead the public when they lump the crime rates for 16 and 17-year-olds together with the much lower crime rates for 12 to 14-year-olds.*

These super-predators lack the normal human desires for affection, companionship, and respect. And unlike other humans, they are impervious to punishment:

> On the horizon, therefore, are tens of thousands of severely morally impoverished juvenile super-predators. . . . They fear neither the stigma of arrest nor the pain of imprisonment. . . . In prison or out, the things that super-predators get by their criminal behavior—sex, drugs, money—are their own immediate rewards. Nothing else matters to them.

The warnings of DiIulio and others formed the intellectual underpinning of the hyper-punitive approach to crime control that led to legislation like Prop. 21 and "Three Strikes" in California. At the national level, DiIulio's terminology was embraced by U.S. Representative Bill McCollum when he introduced a crime bill, the "Violent Youth Predator Act of 1996," which would have required adult prosecution of children as young as thirteen for certain offenses.

Exaggerated claims of youth crime

A coming flood of remorseless young plunderers, killers, and rapists who cannot be deterred or rehabilitated certainly is frightening. But how real is the threat?

Figure 3 shows that homicide arrests in California for offenders under 20 years of age more than doubled between 1986 and 1991.[2] Youth homicide arrests then were cut almost in half between 1991 and 1998.[3]

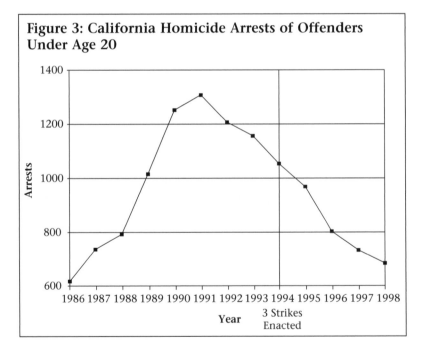

Figure 3: California Homicide Arrests of Offenders Under Age 20

The homicide rate rose and then fell for all youth, but the roller coaster pattern was more pronounced for minorities. Figure 4 shows the relative changes in the youth homicide arrest

2. Six hundred eighteen homicide arrests occurred in 1986, and 1,307 in 1991.
3. Six hundred eighty-three homicide arrests took place in 1998.

rate by ethnic group, setting the 1986 rate for each group equal to 100. For young Whites, the homicide rate rose by 29% from 1986 to 1991 and then dropped by 48% from 1991 to 1998. For young Blacks, the homicide rate peaked in 1990 at a rate 75% above the 1986 level and then dropped by 70% from 1990 to 1998. The rate changes were even more dramatic for young Hispanics. The Hispanic youth homicide rate increased by 196% from 1986 to 1991 and then dropped by 53% from 1991 to 1998. Note that the drop in the homicide rate for each group began several years before the passage of the California Three Strikes law in 1994. The drop in the California youth homicide rate is not unique. Across the nation, offense rates for homicide and for serious crime generally have dropped for youth offenders. In light of these trends, it is hard to justify predictions that the nation stands on the brink of a youth crime explosion.

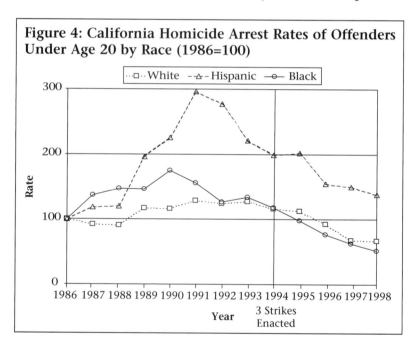

Figure 4: California Homicide Arrest Rates of Offenders Under Age 20 by Race (1986=100)

Inaccurate perceptions of crime and gang threat

Table 1 shows that a majority of the population continued to believe that the crime problem was getting worse years after crime rates began to drop. In 1992, when crime rates were still rising in many areas, eighty-nine percent of the surveyed population believed that crime was getting worse. By 1998, when crime had been dropping for several years in most of the country, the percentage of those polled who believed crime was rising had dropped to fifty-two percent. Still, citizens who believed crime was rising outnumbered those who thought crime was dropping by almost a three to two ratio. And fear of youth crime, fueled by heavily publicized school shootings in Columbine and elsewhere, was rising.

Table 1: Survey of the General Population

	Is There More Crime in the U.S. than There Was a Year Ago, or Less?	
	More	*Less*
1992	89	3
1996	71	15
1997	64	25
1998	52	35

Fear of youth crime often is focused on gangs. Prop. 21, for example, was justified by a "finding" that youth gangs were a growing threat to the safety of the community. In fact, however, crime rates have dropped most rapidly among Black and Latino youth, the demographic groups reputed to be most dominated by youth gangs.[4] This suggests that criminal gang activity was substantially reduced.

The perceptions of law enforcement officials who deal with crime on a daily basis might be expected to be more accurate than those of the general public. Table 2 shows, however, that despite strong evidence that gang crime had been dropping for

Table 2: 1997 National Gang Youth Survey of Law Enforcement Agencies

	Is the Gang Problem in Your Jurisdiction Getting Better or Worse?		
	Getting Worse	*Staying the Same*	*Getting Better*
1995	49%	41%	10%
1997	35%	45%	20%

4. By 1998, homicides by Hispanics in California had dropped fifty-three percent from their 1991 peak. Homicides by Blacks had dropped seventy percent from their 1990 peak.

years, law enforcement agencies were much more likely to believe that the gang problem was getting worse than to believe it was improving.

Demand for "get tough" policies

The belief that youth gangs "pose a unique threat" and have "become more violent, bolder, and better organized" produces a popular demand for "get tough" policies against gang members. The following is only a partial list of such policies.

- The formation of specialized antigang law enforcement units, like the LAPD's CRASH unit, which lies in the center of the police misconduct scandal in the Rampart division.
- Statutes providing for enhanced criminal penalties for crimes committed by gang members.
- Civil injunctions that would enjoin alleged gang members from engaging in ordinarily legal activities such as walking or driving in a car with other alleged gang members.
- Creation of centralized databases of alleged gang members and "associates" for the use of law enforcement officials.
- Police officers stop, question and, if possible, search suspected gang members even if there is no evidence that they are currently committing a crime.

A detailed analysis of these anti-gang policies is beyond the scope of this article. We will examine briefly, however, the impact of gang databases on young minority males.

Targeting youths for gang databases

During the 1990s law enforcement agencies across the nation increasingly made use of computer-based gang databases. These databases contain the lists of alleged gang members and gang associates, together with personal information about each entry. Information entered into a database might include the person's gang membership, gang moniker, home address, identifying marks or tattoos, and even photographs. Remarkably, the information often is gathered from the alleged gang members themselves. Police officers will stop suspected gang members, question them about their gang membership and even take their photographs. Youths stopped and questioned by the police may fear retaliation if they refuse to answer the questions asked or if they deny permission to be photographed.

There are few safeguards against being falsely identified as a gang member. Lists are secret; access is denied to the public. Individuals have no right to know that they have been placed on a list. Police officers are not required to get approval from a judge or magistrate before entering a name on a database. An individual may be entered on a gang database even if he has never been arrested or suspected of a crime. Once entered into a database, it seldom is possible for individuals to get their names removed.

> *The 'Violent Youth Predator Act of 1996'... would have required adult prosecution of children as young as thirteen for certain offenses.*

The criteria for placement on a gang list are broad. One set of guidelines, for example, provides that names should be added to the list only if two or more of the following gang criteria are met:

- Professes to being a gang member.
- Is deemed a gang member by a reliable source, such as a trusted informant, teacher, or parent.
- Is called a gang member by an untested informant with corroboration.
- Has gang graffiti on his personal property or clothing.
- Is observed, by an officer, using gang hand signs.
- Hangs around with gang members.
- Is arrested with gang members.
- Identifies his gang affiliation when brought to county jail.

Some of the criteria have little probative weight. An individual living in an area with a significant gang presence may find it difficult to avoid "hanging around" with gang members. The problem is particularly tricky because an individual may not know which of his neighbors the police regard as gang members. Other criteria are difficult to evaluate. It is hard to assess, for example, the reliability of the information provided by a teacher, parent, or "trusted informant." It is unclear what "corroboration" is needed to verify the statements of an "untested informant." More important, even if the criteria were sound, there is no independent check on whether a police officer has applied the criteria correctly when adding an individual to the database.

The vague criteria, secrecy of the process, and lack of judicial review create a danger that police officers add many young, minority males to the database simply because they wear hip-hop clothing and live in poverty-stricken, high-crime areas. And there is substantial evidence that this is precisely what has occurred in California.

One 1992 study of the Los Angeles gang database found almost half of the Black men in the county between the ages of twenty-one and twenty-four were on some gang list.[5] A more recent examination of the 112,000 purported Los Angeles gang members or associates on the state CAL/GANG database found that 62,000 were entered by specialized LAPD antigang CRASH units, including the unit from the scandal-ridden Rampart division. About two-thirds of the persons entered were Latinos and about one-third were Blacks. Only about 2000 Whites were entered on the gang list.

The LAPD argues that the database is useful in the investigation of crimes committed by gang members. Such tools against gang violence are essential, it is argued, because of the large number of gang-related crimes, defined broadly as any crime with a gang member as a perpetrator or a victim, even if the crime was not connected to a gang purpose. During one recent year, the LAPD noted, gang members committed 7600 offenses, including 136 homicides.

> *It is hard to justify predictions that the nation stands on the brink of a youth crime explosion.*

These crime figures, while not trivial, are small in comparison with the alleged population of 112,000 gang members and associates in Los Angeles County. If the LAPD's figures are correct and there are 7600 gang crimes and 112,000 gang members, only one crime is committed each year for every fifteen gang members or, put differently, the average gang member commits one crime every fifteen years. Unless gang members

5. Similar practices exist elsewhere. In Denver, for example, two-thirds of the young Black men in the city apparently are on the gang database. A reported 3,691 Blacks were on the gang list, a number equivalent to two-thirds of the Black males between twelve and twenty-four in the city.

are a surprisingly law abiding group, the gang database includes many individuals who have ended their gang involvement or who never were gang members in the first place.

There is little doubt that gangs are an important social
problem and that hard-core gang members pose a significant
threat to the safety of the community. But gang databases contain many innocent young minority males, who pose no serious threat to society, together with individuals who are truly
dangerous.

Reinforcing racial discrimination

The burden of the demonization of youth and youth gangs
falls most heavily on minorities, especially young minority
males. The names entered on gang databases are almost exclu-
sively those of minorities. Gang membership is so closely associated with minority youth that in some jurisdictions most of
the young minority males are considered by the police to be
gang members or associates. The close association of gang
membership and minority status permits politicians and com-
mentators to "play the race card" indirectly. Public officials
may be reluctant to endorse a "war against young minority offenders" or "tougher criminal penalties for young minorities"
because of a fear that they will be accused of racism. It is much
safer to endorse a "war against gangs" or "tougher criminal
penalties for gang members." Gangs become a proxy for race.

Targeting minorities for special scrutiny can undermine the
relationship between police and the citizens they serve. As
shown in Table 3, Blacks and Hispanics are more than twice as
likely as Whites to believe that the police in their community
do not treat all races fairly.

Table 3

Do the Police in Your Community Treat All Races Fairly or Do They Tend To Treat One or More of These Groups Unfairly? (1999)		
	Treat all races fairly	*Treat one or more groups unfairly*
White	67	25
Black	30	63
Hispanic	48	52

Demonizing minority youth can create a climate that fosters police misconduct. If young offenders are "super-predators" and if the operation against gangs is a "war," then violating a suspected gang member's constitutional rights or even planting evidence may be viewed as justified. Table 4 shows that Hispanics, and especially Blacks, are far more likely to fear being arrested by the police for a crime they did not commit.

Table 4

Are You Sometimes Afraid That the Police Will Stop and Arrest You When You Are Completely Innocent, or Not? (1999)		
	Yes, sometimes afraid	*No, not afraid*
White	16	84
Black	43	56
Hispanic	28	72

It might be claimed that the burden placed on innocent Blacks and Latinos is outweighed by the benefits of reducing crime. Consider, for example, the use of gang lists to help police in crime investigations by creating a database of nicknames, addresses, photographs, identifying marks, and similar items. Even if many of the people named in the database are innocent of any wrongdoing, it might be argued that the harm to them is small. If they commit no crime, a police investigation will absolve them.

> *If databases of gang members are an effective crime fighting tool, then a database of all citizens would be much more effective.*

Arguments such as these surely underestimate both the burden of being a target of heightened police scrutiny and the likelihood of false conviction. More important, such arguments usually are made by individuals who will never bear such burdens themselves. If databases of gang members are an effective crime fighting tool, then a database of all citizens would be much more effective. The government could take fingerprints, DNA samples, and photographs of all individuals above the age of twelve and enter the information into a national computer system together with each individual's name, address, occupation, and other personal information. With periodic updates, such a database might be a powerful tool in the fight against crime. Most citizens, we suspect, would reject such an invasion of their privacy as repugnant even if such a database would reduce crime.

Underutilization of nonpunitive approaches to crime reduction

Strong criminal sanctions and a high probability of apprehension can help reduce crime. Viewing young offenders as incorrigible super-predators and street hoodlums, however, encourages a focus on law enforcement even when less punitive approaches are a more cost-effective way to reduce crime.

A recent study by [the nonprofit research institution] RAND, for example, found that giving disadvantaged high school students cash and other incentives to graduate was several times more effective in reducing crime, per dollar spent, than the tougher penalties of Three Strikes. Parental training and therapy for families with very young, school-age children who have begun to "act out" in school was also substantially more cost-effective at reducing crime than Three Strikes.

More broadly, demonizing criminal offenders deflects attention away from the responsibility of society to remedy the social and economic conditions that produce a high crime rate in poor urban neighborhoods. Advocates of "get tough" approaches to crime argue that young persons, however disadvantaged, must be held responsible for their wrongdoing. Fair enough. But the privileged adults who control our nation's social policies should be held equally accountable for their failure to address effectively poverty, poor health care, underfunded schools, racial discrimination, and other social conditions that produce high crime rates.

The demonization of youth and especially young minority males fosters abusive police behavior, reinforces racial stereotypes and prevents the adoption of cost-effective, nonpunitive methods of reducing crime. It can also have a devastating impact on innocent, young minority males targeted by police as gang members or associates. Consider for example, the following excerpt from a school essay written by Jesus Daniel Guerrero, a B-student with no history of misconduct who, with an older brother mixed up in gangs, was almost certainly placed on the CAL/GANG database:

> As a child, I would spend countless hours day-dreaming of becoming a mighty police officer. . . . But as I entered my junior high school years . . . my dream of becoming a police officer began to fade like sunlight at dusk. . . . I have been scolded, searched, handcuffed, pushed, kicked and wrong-fully accused of crimes I did not commit.

10

Lack of Brain Development Makes Juveniles Less Culpable than Adults

Adam Ortiz

Adam Ortiz is a policy fellow with the American Bar Association Juvenile Justice Center and works specifically on the elimination of the juvenile death penalty. Previously, he was the deputy director for Amnesty International's Midwest Regional Office, where he led successful campaigns against police brutality, executions of adult and juvenile offenders, and the release of several prisoners of conscience.

Using magnetic resonance imaging, researchers have been able to "map" the brains of children and adults. They have discovered that a naturally occurring "pruning process," which makes the brain's operation more efficient, is not completed until age twenty-one or twenty-two. Because the brains of juveniles, particularly the frontal lobes, are not fully developed, youths lack the ability to perform critical adult functions, such as plan, anticipate consequences, and control impulses. Therefore, it is unreasonable to expect juveniles to make decisions as if they were adults. Combining these deficiencies with the dramatic fluctuations in hormones and emotions experienced in adolescence, criminal behaviors sometimes result. Certain risk factors, including head traumas, domestic violence, substance abuse, poor supervision, and sexual abuse, may trigger violent behaviors that an adolescent brain is poorly equipped to deter. Of-

Adam Ortiz, "Adolescent Brain Development and Legal Culpability," *ABA Fact Sheet*, www.abanet.org, Spring 2003. Copyright © 2002 by ABANet.org. All rights reserved. Reproduced by permission.

ten adolescents outgrow these brain-function deficiencies. Therefore, while juveniles must be punished for their crimes, treating them like adults is patently unreasonable and unfair.

"[T]hey] frequently know the difference between right and wrong and are competent to stand trial. Because of their impairments, however, by definition they have diminished capacities to understand and process mistakes and learn from experience, to engage in logical reasoning, to control impulses, and to understand the reactions of others. . . . Their deficiencies do not warrant an exemption from criminal sanctions, but they do diminish their personal culpability."

This point was made in the *Atkins v. Virginia* Supreme Court decision (2002) that banned the execution of the mentally retarded. As supported by recent scientific research, this argument applies equally to offenders under 18 years of age.

Adolescence is a transitional period of life during which a child is becoming, but is not yet, an adult. An adolescent is at a crossroads of changes, where emotions, hormones, judgment, identity and the physical body are so in flux that expert researchers, as well as parents, struggle to fully understand their impact.

As a society, we recognize the limitations of adolescents and restrict their privilege to drive, drink alcohol, smoke, vote, marry, enter into contracts, and even watch "R"-rated movies. Each year we spend billions of dollars for drug prevention and sex education to protect youth during this vulnerable time. Thus, when it comes to capital punishment, society is guilty of a critical contradiction when we subject adolescent offenders to the death penalty.

The adolescent brain

Along with everything else in the body, the brain changes significantly during adolescence. In the last five years, scientists have discovered that adolescent brains are far less developed than previously believed.

The human brain has been called the most complex three-pound mass in the known universe—and for good reason—it has literally billions of connections among its parts.

The largest part of the brain is called the frontal lobe. A small area of the frontal lobe called the prefrontal cortex, located behind the forehead, controls the most advanced functions. This part, often referred to as the "CEO" of the body, provides us with our advanced level of consciousness. It allows us to prioritize thoughts, imagine, think in the abstract, anticipate consequences, plan, and control impulses.

Brain development

Researchers at UCLA, Harvard Medical School and the National Institute of Mental Health have teamed up in a massive project to "map" the development of the brain from childhood to adulthood.

These scientists are utilizing advances in magnetic resonance imaging (MRI) which provides three-dimensional images of the body without the use of radiation (as in an x-ray). This breakthrough allows scientists to scan children safely numerous times over many years.

What came as a surprise to scientists was the discovery that the brain undergoes an intense overproduction of gray matter (the tissue that does the "thinking") during adolescence. Then, a period of "pruning" takes over, where gray matter is shed and discarded.

This process is similar to pruning the branches of a tree: cutting branches in some places stimulates growth overall.

The pruning process has been described as a "massive loss of brain tissue" by Paul Thompson, a member of the UCLA research team. Tissue is lost at a rate of 1 to 2% per year.

> *The frontal lobe undergoes the most change during adolescence—by far. It is also the last part of the brain to develop.*

The pruning process is accompanied by myelination, a process in which the brain's white matter, or "insulation," focuses, refines and makes the brain's operation more efficient. The pace and severity of these changes, which continue until one's early 20s, have been carefully scrutinized by researchers. These changes mean that the brain is still developing.

Dr. Elizabeth Sowell, a member of the UCLA brain research team, has led studies of brain development from adolescence to adulthood (roughly ages 12 through 22). She writes that the frontal lobe undergoes the most change during adolescence—by far. It is also the last part of the brain to develop.

Both the pruning and the insulation process are critical to the brain's development. Insulation affects the speed and quality of brain activity while pruning and the development of gray matter contribute to overall cognitive functioning, including the ability to reason effectively.

Biology and behavior

These correlations are providing new perspectives to the old question: "Why do teens behave the way they do?"

The answers to this question have widespread implications in the fields of education, mental illness, and juvenile justice, and were the centerpiece of a May 2000 White House Conference titled "Raising Responsible and Resourceful Youth."

> *It's sort of unfair to expect them to have adult levels of organizational skills or decision making before their brain is finished being built.*

Jay Giedd, the lead researcher on the subject at the National Institute of Mental Health, explained to PBS's *Frontline* that during adolescence the "part of the brain that is helping organization, planning and strategizing is not done being built yet. . . . It's sort of unfair to expect them to have adult levels of organizational skills or decision making before their brain is finished being built."

Connections to disorders and culpability

Dr. Deborah Yurgelun-Todd of Harvard Medical School is one of the chief researchers on the relation between brain development and cognitive deficiencies. She says that the underdevelopment of the frontal lobe makes adolescents "more prone to react with 'gut instinct'." She says that the tendency to use the part of the brain called the amygdala (responsible for 'gut reactions') instead of the prefrontal cortex (responsible for reasoning) continues until adulthood, when individuals are able to respond more maturely.

MRI scans have shown that even the most sophisticated-appearing teenagers rely heavily on the amygdala, an instinctual part of the brain. Also, males use these 'instinctual' parts of the brain much more than females as the male frontal lobe develops more slowly than that of the female's.

> *There is now biological evidence that adolescents do not have the same ability as adults to make sound decisions and to prevent impulsive behavior.*

Dr. Ruben C. Gur, neuropsychologist and Director of the Brain Behavior Laboratory at the University of Pennsylvania, explains that the frontal lobe is "involved in behavioral facets germane to many aspects of criminal culpability. Perhaps most relevant is the involvement of these brain regions in the control of aggression and other impulses. . . . If the neural substrates of these behaviors have not reached maturity before adulthood, it is unreasonable to expect the behaviors themselves to reflect mature thought processes."

Simply put, there is now biological evidence that adolescents do not have the same ability as adults to make sound decisions and to prevent impulsive behavior.

Dr. Gut writes: "The evidence now is strong that the brain does not cease to mature until the early 20s in those relevant parts that govern impulsivity, judgment, planning for the future, foresight of consequences, and other characteristics that make people morally culpable. . . . Indeed, age 21 or 22 would be closer to the 'biological' age of maturity."

Other changes in the body

In addition to the profound physical changes of the brain, adolescents also undergo dramatic hormonal and emotional changes.

One of the hormones having the most dramatic effect on the body is testosterone, closely associated with aggression, which increases its levels tenfold.

Emotionally, an adolescent "is really both part child and part adult," according to professor and author Melvin Lewis.

Normal emotional development includes a period of self-searching, where the adolescent tries to grow out of the child. This involves a conflict between building identity and facing childlike insecurities. The well-known behaviors associated with this process include self-absorption, a powerful need for privacy, mood swings, dressing uniquely, and participating in forms of escapism such as video games, music, talking on the phone, and riskier behaviors such as using drugs or engaging in sexual activity.

Development and delinquency

The turmoil often associated with these changes sometimes results in poor decisions and desperate behaviors.

Studies find that 20 to 30 percent of high school students consider suicide, and that suicide is the third-leading cause of death among teenagers, occurring once every two hours—well over 4,000 times a year, according to the US Surgeon General.

Running away from home is also common, as the General Accounting Office estimates 1.3 million kids are on the street each year.

The US Office of National Drug Control Policy estimates that 10.8 percent of persons between ages 12 and 18 used an illicit drug "in the past month" (well above the national average of 7.1 percent of the population at large) and nearly a third of adolescents used alcohol.

Also, illegal acts are more common during adolescence than during any other time of life. Estimates of the proportion of males who have been arrested before the age of 18 hover around 25%. This peak in criminal activity during adolescence is "quite stable across different social contexts" and "is present in all of the cultures studied to date."

Triggers

Research also shows that certain stressful experiences can trigger violent behavior, like a spark to flammable material. The American Academy of Pediatrics has identified several risk factors that can trigger violence in adolescents including being witness to domestic violence or substance abuse within the family, being poorly or inappropriately supervised, and being the victim of physical or sexual assault, among other things.

It should come as no surprise that juveniles who commit

murder come from environments rife with these triggers. In 1987, Dr. Dorothy Otnow Lewis of New York University led comprehensive diagnostic evaluations of 14 juveniles on death row (at that time, 40 percent) in four states. She found that nine had major neuropsychological disorders and seven had psychotic disorders since early childhood. Twelve reported having been brutally abused physically or sexually, and five reported having been sodomized by relatives.

> *Estimates of the proportion of males who have been arrested before the age of 18 hover around 25%. This peak in criminal activity . . . 'is present in all of the cultures studied to date.'*

Other common characteristics included suffering trauma to the head and IQ scores under 90 (only two did better). Only three had average reading abilities, and another three had learned to read on death row. Lewis also found that many of these dysfunctions were not presented to juries due to poor representation or the juvenile withholding or downplaying these facts out of embarrassment or bad judgment.

Dr. Lewis' primary findings were later corroborated by Robinson and Stephens (1992). They found that two thirds of all juveniles sentenced to death had backgrounds of abuse, profound psychological disturbances, low IQ, indigence, and/or intensive substance abuse.

Lessened culpability

New scientific research confirms that adolescence is a time of transition. The adolescent is not an adult, and is subject to great limitations in judgment and maturity.

For social and biological reasons, teens have increased difficulty making mature decisions and understanding the consequences of their actions. Research suggests that these limitations persist until the early 20s.

Often, adolescents *grow out of* these less mature ways of dealing with problems, including destructive behavior. Studies show that more than half of all youths that pass through the juvenile justice system do not return.

This understanding does not excuse adolescents from punishments for violent crime, but it dearly lessens their culpability. This is the premise beneath society's across-the-board restrictions on voting rights, alcohol and tobacco consumption and serving in the armed forces. Indeed, this is why we refer to those under 18 as "minors" and "juveniles"—because, in so many respects they are *less than adult.*

Therefore, the death penalty for juveniles is a grave contradiction, and is contrary to our most fundamental notions of fairness, which accords punishment according to culpability.

The [American Bar Association] urges all state legislatures to ban this practice at the earliest opportunity.

Organizations to Contact

The editors have compiled the following list of organizations concerned with the issues debated in this book. The descriptions are derived from materials provided by the organizations. All have publications or information available for interested readers. The list was compiled on the date of publication of the present volume; names, addresses, phone and fax numbers, and e-mail addresses may change. Be aware that many organizations take several weeks or longer to respond to inquiries, so allow as much time as possible.

American Bar Association Juvenile Justice Center
740 Fifteenth St. NW, 10th Floor, Washington, DC 20005-1009
(202) 662-1506 • fax: (202) 662-1501
Web site: www.abanet.org/crimjust/juvjust

The goal of the American Bar Association Juvenile Justice Center is to advance the juvenile defense bar through training, technical assistance, information dissemination, and advocacy. The center works to improve access to counsel and the quality of representation for children in the juvenile justice system. Among its publications is *More than Meets the Eye: Rethinking Assessment, Competency, and Sentencing for a Harsher Era of Juvenile Justice*. Its Web site maintains links to a multitude of student resources.

Center on Juvenile and Criminal Justice (CJCJ)
National Office, 1622 Folsom St., San Francisco, CA 94103
(415) 621-5661 • fax: (415) 621-5466
Web site: www.cjcj.org

The CJCJ is a private, nonprofit organization advocating reduced reliance on incarceration as a solution to social problems. The center provides direct services, technical assistance, and policy research in the criminal justice field. The *CJCJ Justice Policy Journal* includes articles on juvenile justice, including "Juvenile Crime, Adult Adjudication, and the Death Penalty: Draconian Policies Revisited," and publications available online include *The Color of Justice: An Analysis of Juvenile Adult Court Transfers in California for the Building Blocks for Youth Initiative*.

Council of Juvenile Correctional Administrators (CJCA)
170 Forbes Rd., Suite 106, Braintree, MA 02184
(781) 843-1688
Web site: www.cjca.net

CJCA is dedicated to improving youth correctional services and practices through the exchange of ideas among correction system administrators. It seeks to educate the public about juvenile justice and corrections, with emphasis on treatment and rehabilitation. CJCA publishes a quarterly newsletter for members, maintains a Web site, cooperates in research projects, and publishes position papers, including *Waiver and Transfer.*

Criminal Justice Legal Foundation (CJLF)
PO Box 1199, Sacramento, CA 95816
(916) 446-0345
e-mail: cjlf@cjlf.org • Web site: www.cjlf.org

The CJLF is a nonprofit, public interest organization dedicated to balancing the rights of crime victims and the criminally accused. The foundation's purpose is to assure that people who are guilty of committing crimes receive swift and certain punishment in an orderly and thoroughly constitutional manner. To that end its attorneys introduce scholarly friend of the court briefs in criminal cases before state and federal courts of appeals. Publications include the quarterly newsletter *Advisory*, and *Should California's Three-Strikes Law Be Weakened or Eliminated?*

Joint Center for Poverty Research (JCPR)
Northwestern University, Institute for Policy Research
2046 Sheridan Rd., Evanston, IL 60208
(847) 491-4145 • fax: (847) 467-2459
University of Chicago, Harris Graduate School of Public Policy Studies
1155 E. Sixtieth St., Chicago, IL 60637
(773) 702-0472 • fax: (773) 702-0926
Web site: www.jcpr.org

The JCPR is a national, interdisciplinary academic research center that seeks to advance understanding of the effects of poverty in America, including high rates of juvenile crime. Through social science research, the center attempts to influence the discussion and formation of policy, and the behavior and beliefs of individuals and organizations. Publications available include *Should Juvenile Offenders Be Tried as Adults?*

Justice Policy Institute
4455 Connecticut Ave. NW, Suite B-500, Washington, DC 20008
(202) 363-7847 • fax: (202) 363-8677
e-mail: info@justicepolicy.org • Web site: www.justicepolicy.org

The Justice Policy Institute is a think tank committed to reducing society's reliance on incarceration. It generates pragmatic approaches to problems within both juvenile and criminal justice systems. A collection of reports located on its Web site includes *The Florida Experiment*, a study of trying juveniles as adults in Florida.

Juvenile Law Center
The Philadelphia Building
1315 Walnut St., 4th Floor, Philadelphia, PA 19107
(215) 625-0551 • (800) 875-8887
fax: (215) 625-2808 • Web site: www.jlc.org

The Juvenile Law Center works to ensure that the child welfare, juvenile justice, and other public systems provide vulnerable children with the protection and services they need to become happy, healthy, and productive adults. The center distributes a wide range of publications, testifies at public forums, advises the executive and legislative branches of state and federal governments on the effects of proposed legislation or regulations on children, serves as a resource to the media, and answers inquiries from the general public. Its Web site offers links to a broad range of articles and reports on juvenile justice issues.

National Center for Juvenile Justice
710 Fifth Ave., Suite 3000, Pittsburgh, PA 15219
(412) 227-6950 • fax: (412) 227-6955
Web site: www.ncjj.org

The National Center for Juvenile Justice is a private, nonprofit research organization dedicated to the improvement of the juvenile and family court system. Founded in 1973, the center compiles statistics and conducts and sponsors independent and original research on topics related directly and indirectly to the field of juvenile justice. Publications available include *Trying and Sentencing Juveniles as Adults.*

National Center on Institutions and Alternatives (NCIA)
7222 Ambassador Rd., Baltimore, MD 21244
(410) 265-1490 • fax: (410) 597-9656
Web site: www.ncia.org

The NCIA promotes innovative concepts in criminal and juvenile justice, providing professional research, training, and technical assistance in support of alternative, community-based programs for nonviolent criminal offenders. The center's services focus on four major areas: criminal justice, mental health, education, and advocacy. Publications include *An Analysis of Juvenile Homicides: Where They Occur and the Effectiveness of Adult Court Intervention* and an online newsletter, *Criminal Defense Update.*

Office of Juvenile Justice and Delinquency Prevention (OJJDP)
810 Seventh St. NW, Washington, DC 20531
(202) 307-5911 • fax: (202) 307-2093
e-mail: askjj@ncjrs.org • Web site: http://ojjdp.ncjrs.org

The OJJDP was established by the Juvenile Justice and Delinquency Prevention Act of 2002. Its missions are (1) to support state and local programs that prevent delinquent behavior, (2) to promote public safety by encouraging accountability for acts of juvenile delinquency, and (3) to assist state and local governments in addressing juvenile crime through technical assistance, research, training, evaluation, and the dissemination of information. Among other publications, the agency publishes the newsletter *OJJDP News @ a Glance*, fact sheets, bulletins, and a periodic publication, *Juvenile Justice.*

Youth Law Center
Children's Legal Protection Center
1010 Vermont Ave. NW, Suite 310, Washington, DC 20005
(202) 637-0377 • fax: (202) 379-1600
e-mail: info@youthlawcenter.com • Web site: www.youthlawcenter.com

The Youth Law Center works to ensure that vulnerable children are provided with the conditions and services they need to grow into healthy, productive adults. Its publications, catalogued on its Web site, address the topics of juvenile justice and youth rights, including *Youth on Trial: A Developmental Perspective on Juvenile Justice.*

Bibliography

Books

James Austin, Kelly Dedel Johnson, and Maria Gregoriou	*Juveniles in Adult Prisons and Jails: A National Assessment.* Washington, DC: Bureau of Justice Assistance, 2000.
Peter T. Elikann	*Superpredators: The Demonization of Our Children by the Law.* Reading, MA: Perseus, 1999.
R. Barri Flowers	*Kids Who Commit Adult Crimes: Serious Criminality by Juvenile Offenders.* New York: Haworth, 2002.
Thomas Grisso and Robert G. Schwartz, eds.	*Youth on Trial: A Developmental Perspective on Juvenile Justice.* Chicago: University of Chicago Press, 2000.
Human Rights Watch	*Children in Maryland's Jails.* New York: Human Rights Watch, 1999.
Michael D. Keller	*When Good Kids Kill.* Westport, CT: Praeger, 1998.
Michael Mello	*Deathwork: Defending the Condemned.* Minneapolis: University of Minnesota Press, 2002.
Paul E. Tracy	*Decision Making and Juvenile Justice: An Analysis of Bias in Case Processing.* Westport, CT: Praeger, 2002.
U.S. Congress, House Committee on Education and the Workforce, Subcommittee on Select Education	*H.R. 1900, the Juvenile Crime Control and Delinquency Prevention Act of 2001: Hearing Before the Subcommittee on Select Education of the Committee on Education and the Workforce, House of Representatives, One Hundred Seventh Congress, First Session, Hearing Held in Washington, DC, June 6, 2001.* Washington, DC: Government Printing Office, 2002.
Kenneth Wooden	*Weeping in the Playtime of Others: America's Incarcerated Children.* Columbus: Ohio State University Press, 2000.

Periodicals

Jeffrey A. Butts and Adele V. Harrell	"One-Size-Fits-All Justice Simply Isn't Fair," *Christian Science Monitor*, December 1, 1998.
Jeffrey A. Butts and Ojmarrh Mitchell	"Brick by Brick: Dismantling the Border Between Juvenile and Adult Justice," *Criminal Justice*, 2000.
Paul D'Amato	"The Color of Justice," *International Socialist Review*, June/July 2000.

John J. DiIulio   "The Coming of the Super-Predators," *Weekly Standard*, November 27, 1995.

Patricia Edmonds   "A Child No More," *Children's Beat*, Spring 2003.

Emily Gaarder and   "Tenuous Borders: Girls Transferred to Adult
Joanne Belknap   Court," *Criminology*, August 2002.

Jean Guccione and   "Activists Want Boys Out of Men's Jail," *Los
Greg Krikorian   Angeles Times*, June 20, 2003.

Rodger Jackson and   "Race and Treating Other People's Children as
Edward Pabon   Adults: Transfer of Juvenile Offenders to Adult
                         Courts," *Journal of Criminal Justice*, November/
                         December 2000.

Elizabeth A. Klug   "Geographical Disparities Among Trying and Sen-
                         tencing Juveniles," *Corrections Today*, December
                         2001.

Murray Levine et al.   "Is It Inherently Prejudicial to Try a Juvenile as an
                         Adult?" *Behavioral Sciences and the Law*, vol. 19,
                         2001.

Patrick T. McCormick   "Fit to Be Tried? Legislators Have Been Making It
                         Easier to Punish Juveniles as Adults," *America*, Feb-
                         ruary 11, 2002.

Eugene A. Moore   "A Community Problem," *Detroit Free Press*, Janu-
                         ary 14, 2000.

Karen S. Peterson   "Public Clamors: Get Tough at a Tender Age," *USA
                         Today*, September 29, 1998.

Richard E. Redding   "Examining Legal Issues: Juvenile Offenders in
                         Criminal Court and Adult Prison," *Corrections To-
                         day*, April 1999.

Marc Schindler and   "The Increased Prosecution of Adolescents in the
Joyce A. Arditti   Adult Criminal Justice System: Impacts on Youth,
                         Family, and Community," *Marriage and Family Re-
                         view*, vol. 32, 2002.

Laurence Steinberg   "Should Juvenile Offenders Be Tried as Adults?"
                         Temple University and John D. and Catherine T.
                         MacArthur Foundation Research Network, January
                         19, 2000.

Lawrence Winner   "The Transfer of Juveniles to Criminal Court:
et al.   Reexamining Recidivism over the Long Term,"
                         Crime and Delinquency, October 1997.

Internet Sources

Carissa Caramanis   "Youth Among Us: Addressing Youthful Offend-
                         ers," February 22, 1999. www.corrections.com.

Fiona Morgan   "Crime School: Does Prosecuting Teenagers as
                         Adults Make Society Safer?" May 26, 1999.
                         www.salon.com.

Index

adjudication proceedings, 42
adult criminal court
  concerns on treatment of youth in, 63
  fairness to minority youth in, 70–71
  juvenile court vs., 10–11, 54–55
  see also transfer, to adult court
African American youth. See minority youth
Altonaga, Cecilia, 15
Amnesty International, 22
And Justice for Some: Differential Treatment of Minority Youth in the Justice System (report), 57, 58
Arizona, 54
Ashcroft, John, 72

Bagley, Jerald, 15, 21
bail, for minority youth, 62–63
Beres, Linda S., 77
Bishop, Donna M., 20, 49, 51, 52, 55
Botkin, Leon, 16, 17, 19
Brazill, Nathaniel, 18, 19
Building Blocks for Youth (report), 58
Bush v. Gore, 15, 19

CAL/GANG database, 87
California
  gang database in, 87–88
  homicide arrests in, 82–83
  sentencing practices in, 12
  trying juveniles in adult court in, 8
Clary, Mike, 14
Collier, Linda J., 39
CRASH unit (Community Response to Street Hoodlums), 77–78, 85, 87
Crist, Victor D., 16

Davis, Brent, 39–40, 43–44
death penalty, 12, 93
DiIulio, John, 8, 81–82
direct file, 9, 17
  percentage of cases filed in, 66
  state attorney's discretion and, 21

Eunick, Tiffany, 25

Fagan, Jeffrey, 51
felonies
  minority over-representation of,

63–64, 65, 66
  transfer of juveniles to adult court and, 9–10, 16
Florida
  juveniles held in adult jails in, 47–48
  juvenile transfers in, 16–17
  challenges to, 15–16
  prosecutorial, 9
  study on deterrent effects of, 52–53
  tough-on-juveniles reputation of, 14–16
  wrong approach of, to accused juvenile offenders, 17–19
Florida Department of Juvenile Justice study, 20
foster care, 41–42
Frazier, Charles E., 20

gangs
  associated with minority youth, 88
  databases on, 85–88, 89–90
  "get tough" policies against, 85
  inaccurate perceptions about, 84–85
  threat to public of, 78–79
Gang Violence and Juvenile Crime Prevention Act (1998), 78–80
Golden, Andrew, 39
Gorski, Terence T., 22
Griffith, Thomas D., 77
Gur, Ruben C., 96

Hall, Darryl Dayan, 72–73
Hansen, Brian, 45
Huffington, Arianna, 9

Idaho, 50–51
Illinois, 41
incarceration
  adult prisons
    juvenile prisons vs., 12–13
    number of Florida children in, 17
    physical and sexual abuse in, 22–23
    problems for juveniles in, 47–48
    effect of transfer laws on, 51–52
    lack of training for correctional officers for, 47
    lack of adult/juvenile segregation

for, 46
of minority youth, 67, 69–70
Ingley, Stephen, 46–47

Johnson, Mitchell, 39
Jonesboro school shootings, 39–40
judicial waiver, 9
    in Florida, 17
    increase in, 53
    judges' discretion for, 53–54
Juszkiewicz, Jolanta, 56
juvenile crime
    crime-prone ages for, 79–80
    claims about
        exaggerated, 82–83
        using, to justify Proposition 21,
            78–79
    inaccurate perceptions about,
        83–84
    increase in, 40–41, 72–73
    invoking fears about, 8, 46, 81–82
juvenile justice system
    adult criminal justice system vs.,
        10–11, 54–55
    history of, 56–57
    increase of waived cases in, 53
    is ill-equipped for serious crime,
        74–75
    is not effective, 41–43
    three critical principles of, 23–24
juvenile offenders
    federal prosecution of, 43–44
    Florida's wrong approach to
        accused, 17–19
    government failure in protecting
        public from, 73–74
    legislation providing tough
        measures on, 74, 75–76, 78–79
    nonpunitive approaches to, 90
    treated as children vs. criminals,
        39–40
    triggers causing violent behavior
        by, 97–98
juveniles
    brain development of, 92–95
    hormonal and emotional changes
        in, 96–97
    instinctual behavior by, 95–96
    lessened culpability for, 98–99
    poor decisions and delinquent
        behavior by, 97
    sanctioning, as adults
        brain development of youth and,
            92–93
        in California, 8
        examples of, 45–46
        fairness to minority youth and,
            59

federal reform for, 75–76
    in Florida, 14
    increase in juvenile crime and,
        81–82
    is an effective tool, 75
    is immoral, 22–26
    states supporting, 41
    support for, 28–30, 43–44
    study showing, 30–38
    uniform minimum age is needed
        for, 43
    see also transfer, to adult court

Kanka, Megan, 43
Kansas, 41
King, Alex, 18
King, Derek, 18
Krischer, Barry E., 45–46
Kupchik, Aaron, 49, 51–52, 55

Lane, Jodi, 20
Lanza-Kaduce, Lonn, 20
Laster, Anthony, 45–46
Latino youth. See minority youth
Lewis, Dorothy Otnow, 98

mandatory sentencing, 12
mandatory transfer, 9
Martinez, Jose, 8
McCollum, Bill, 8, 82
Mears, Daniel P., 27
Megan's Law, 43
Michigan, 11
Miller, David C., 15
Minnesota, 11
minority youth
    changes in homicide arrest rate
        among, 82–83
    charges filed against, 64–65
    criminal court's disparate treatment
        of, 62–63, 70–71
    cumulative disadvantage of, 57–58
    decrease in crime by, 84
    demonization of, 77, 88, 90–91
    disproportionately receive transfers
        to adult court, 19
    felony arrests of, 63–64, 65, 66
    impact of gang databases on,
        85–87, 89–90
    judicial waiver is biased against, 9
    legal representation for, 69
    pretrial release and detention of,
        65–69
    prosecution of, vs. of white youth,
        68–69
    sentences for, 69–70
    study on prosecution of, 58–62
    unfair police conduct against,

77–78, 88–89
Montana, 50–51
Myers, Michael, 48

National Opinion Survey of Crime
     and Justice (NOSCJ), 30
New Jersey, 51–52
New York, 43, 50, 51–52

Ortiz, Adam, 92

parens patriae, 27, 36
Pennsylvania, 43, 53
police, unfair treatment of minority
     youth by, 77–78, 88–89, 91
presumptive transfer, 10
prison. *See* incarceration
Proposition 21, 78–81, 84
prosecutorial transfers, 9, 18
punishment
     failure of, 24
     juvenile justice system is ineffective
          at, 41–43
     juvenile vs. adult criminal court
          gap in, 52
     philosophy of, impacting support
          for trying juveniles as adults,
          33–38
     see also incarceration

recidivism
     adult court sentences increase, 18,
          20
     impact of juvenile transfers on,
          50–53, 55
rehabilitation programs
     children deserve, 23
     preferred over adult court, 19
     public support for, 28, 29
     types of people supporting, 29
Reyna, Jose Carlos, 20–21
Rosenbaum, Richard, 18–19
Rosenblatt, Joel D., 16, 21

school shootings, 39–40
Schwartz, I.M., 28–29
sentencing practices, 11
     in adult vs. juvenile court, 52
     for minority youth, 69–70
     problematic, 12
     see also juveniles, sanctioning, as
          adults
Serious Habitual Offender
     Comprehensive Program

(SHOCAP), 74
Shorstein, Harry, 49
Simple City Crew (gang), 73
Snyder, Howard, 49, 53
Soule, Chris, 48
South Carolina, 54
Sowell, Elizabeth, 94–95
State Court Processing Statistics
     (SCPS), 59–60
states
     changes in juvenile crime policy
          by, 41, 57
     differences in juvenile transfer
          policies among, 8–9
     differing in sentencing practices,
          11–12
     options for juvenile transfers for,
          9–10
     statutory exclusion provision, 9–10,
          66

Tate, Lionel, 18–19, 25–26
three-strikes law, 12
Timmendequas, Jesse, 43
transfer, to adult court
     deterrent effect of, 50–53
     fairness to minority youth and,
          58–59
     judges hesitate on, 54
     legal and constitutional challenges
          to, 15–16, 19–21
     mechanisms for, 9–10
     over-representation of minority
          youth for, 57–58
     policy questions on, 49–50
     runs counter to public opinion,
          27–28
     states differing in, 8–9
Triola, Frank P., 14–15, 17, 18, 19–20
Turpin, James, 47

Utah, 54

Violent and Repeat Offender Act
     (1997), 74
Violent Youth Predator Act (1996),
     82
Virginia, 41

waivers. *See* judicial waiver
Wyoming, 50–51

Young, David H., 15